THE CHANGELING

JOY WILLIAMS

THE CHANGELING

30TH *Anniversary Edition*

WITH A FOREWORD BY RICK MOODY

FAIRY TALE REVIEW · PRESS

TUSCALOOSA · 2008

FAIRY TALE REVIEW PRESS
gratefully acknowledges the generosity of The University of Alabama
and other anonymous donors in supporting our mission.

EDITOR: Kate Bernheimer
ART DIRECTION: Jason Johnson & Eli Queen
EDITORIAL ASSISTANTS 2007-2008: Christopher Hellwig & Andy Johnson

FAIRY TALE REVIEW PRESS
Department of English · University of Alabama
Tuscaloosa AL 35487

WWW.FAIRYTALEREVIEW.COM

Cover Art: "El Perro Semihundido" (1820) by Francisco Goya
reprinted by permission of Museo Nacional del Prado (Madrid, España).

30TH ANNIVERSARY REPRINT EDITION

ISBN: 978-0-9799954-0-8

Library of Congress Cataloguing in Publication Data:
The Changeling / Joy Williams – 30TH Anniversary Edition

FAIRY TALE REVIEW PRESS

*"There are fairy tales to be written for adults,
fairy tales almost blue."*
—ANDRE BRETON

Fairy Tale Review Press is dedicated to helping raise public awareness of the literary and cultural influence of fairy tales, and to appreciating their power and depth as an art form. It celebrates fairy tales as one of our oldest and most underestimated pleasures. Fairy Tale Review Press seeks to improve the critical understanding of new works sewn from fairy tales, and welcomes the public to revisit old tales across borders and time, to celebrate their transfixing power and protect them for future generations of readers. Fairy Tale Review Press also publishes Fairy Tale Review, an annual journal. Fairy Tale Review Press invites your letters and comments.

Please write to FAIRYTALEREVIEW@GMAIL.COM

BOOKS BY JOY WILLIAMS

Novels

STATE OF GRACE

THE CHANGELING

BREAKING AND ENTERING

THE QUICK AND THE DEAD

Story Collections

ESCAPES

TAKING CARE

HONORED GUEST

Non-Fiction

ILL NATURE

THE FLORIDA KEYS

For Rust

ACKNOWLEDGEMENT

I am very grateful to Yaddo, to the Guggenheim Foundation, and to the National Foundation for the Arts for their assistance.

JOY WILLIAMS

FOREWORD

Second novels! Such accursed children! Even when the writers of them are the best and most talented of writers! As Joy Williams assuredly is! Her first novel, *State of Grace,* was published in 1972 and it had a notable impact from the outset, garnering a nomination for the National Book Award. Williams's prose, in this debut, was possessed of startling luminosity, of twists and turns of such ferocity that she seemed to entrap the world entire in each and every paragraph—as if by assembling all possible perceptions and all opposing points of view. Her interests were dark, even despairing, her people were afflicted, but a romantic's belief in imagination and language seemed, from the first, to indicate a bona fide way out.

The Changeling, which you have before you, followed six years later. Is it possible that the times had changed so dramatically in those years? *The Changeling,* which is rich with the arresting improbabilities of magic realism, with the surrealism of the folkloric revival (Angela Carter's *The Bloody Chamber* was published about the same time), and with the modernist foreboding of *Under the Volcano,* would have seemed perfectly legible in 1973 when *Gravity's Rainbow* was published, or Gaddis's *J.R.* But the late seventies, with their punk rock nihilism and their Studio 54 fatuousness, were perhaps not properly situated to understand this variety of challenge. To their shame.

Thirty years later, the situation looks quite different. Felicitously so. The Joy Williams who went on to write the astonishing short stories of *Taking Care, Escapes,* and *Honored Guest,* and such marvels of realistic other-worldliness as her recent novel *The Quick and the Dead* (2002), has instructed us, as the most original writers must, as to the consumption of her graceful arabesques. The tectonic movement of her paragraphs and her narratives no longer looks impulsive, if indeed it ever did. Now it looks exactly like originality.

The Changeling is chiefly concerned with the lucky and unlucky fortunes of a drink-afflicted young woman called Pearl (and the resonances with the identically named urchin of Hawthorne's *Scarlett Letter* don't seem out of place, summoning up as they do the Gothic scaffolding of that romance). Pearl, who works hard to escape the clutches of a sinister extended family on an island enclave of the Northeast, nonetheless, after surviving a plane crash, finds herself back in the domestic fold, desperately looking for another method of egress, while the feral children of the island gather around her. Among them is her own estranged son, Sam, who may or may not have been swapped with an even more wild child in the disorderly aftermath of her aeronautical accident.

You wouldn't have to look far in Stith Thompson's *Motif-Index of Folk-Literature* to find the immemorial origins of a story like this. More so than in her later work, *The Changeling* welcomes parabolical resonances, citing, e.g., the *Scheherazade* in its course as if to alert us. Yet, as fans of the later Williams will recognize, resolution is too easily come by in much contemporary literature, as in some fairy tales, and so the plot is not the primary compass given us here. Readers who want to know *what happens* will find themselves forced to sit back, relax, etc. As ever with Williams, the book accomplishes its feats more thoroughly through the singularity of its language:

"Pearl's life had never lacked in gesture but it had always avoided significance. It avoided meaning as the bird does the snare. Nothing in her life had prepared Pearl for significance. Each moment that occurred lay mute within her, a buried stone, contained from and irrelevant to herself, an event with neither premonition nor consequence. She couldn't imagine incorporating what was determined as yesterday into what was considered tomorrow."

Or, in describing Pearl's brother-in-law, Lincoln:

"Once he had been a mathematician, a professor at a small university. He found his art, which depended upon the concept of nothing, congenial to his life in general. Numbers pure as light. An order of the universe. Three the masculine, four the feminine, seven the eyes of God. Shelly had been in one of his classes and he considered her to be the dumbest of the lot. She returned her papers blank. Only a few smudges and loops of hair to indicate the vast deserted regions of her brain."

Or, in delineating the effects of the plane crash:

"Even an infant has to be affected by a moment of horror, a moment when all around in a stinking swamp people were metamorphosing into so much meat and probate."

If the characters of this uncanny masque have aspects of the archetypal about them, having been composed in a time when a Jungian symbolisms were in less disrepute, that is no inhibitor to the narrator, who meanwhile ranges freely in a not-so-limited third person, a voice at once elevated and colloquial, melancholy, obscene, and elegiac, both in Pearl's consciousness and above and beyond it. It's hard to read a page of *The Changeling* without coming upon a sentence you want to jot down or memorize, and I could fill the entire introduction with passages of literary delight. Introductory pragmatism forbids such things.

Therefore, a brief word instead about alcoholism. (Yes, the first sentence of the novel is: "There was a young woman sitting in the bar.") Pearl's confinement, as the paragraphs of the novel accrue, is not just upon the island of frigid Protestants. It is also a confinement in the rigors of drink. It's possible, I'd argue, to arrive at reading of *The Changeling* in which the fabulistic occurrences are the result of the impairment, of the gin-and-tonic-around-the-clock which is the besetting misery of this heroine. Such an interpretation would be, I suspect, a bit reductive, but at the same time it's hard not to feel that Pearl's fortunes would be improved by a week locked in a facility wherein she could be kept from hurting herself.

Williams's surpassing mastery as a writer is to see the truth of such a predicament and to wait. There's no judgment of Pearl. There is, on the contrary, an anatomizing of the mess of her circumstances. The appearances of insects in profusion, children in masks, unexplained death and destruction, these are all part of this anatomizing, which is all the more exacting for the specificity and countervailing lucidity of its *words*.

It's the second time through the batting order, they say, when a pitcher's mettle is tested. The batters have seen the arsenal of possibilities, and they begin to feast. Such is the doomed legacy of the second novel. We know what we think of this writer! And we don't want to be surprised! Well, *The Changeling* is nothing if not a surprising book, a parable and a cautionary tale written in a language so virtuosic that it ought to be inscribed on tablets. With this new edition, *The Changeling* is likely to garner a more generous helping of the respect it has, for thirty years, richly deserved.

RICK MOODY
Fishers Island, NY

Further than blood or than bones,
further than bread;
beyond wines, conflagrations,
you come flying.

You come flying, alone, in your solitude,
alone with the dead,
alone in eternity,
shadowless, nameless, you come flying
without sweets, or a mouth, or a thicket of roses,
you come flying.

PABLO NERUDA

THE CHANGELING

First published by Doubleday & Company, Inc.
Garden City, New York 1978

CHAPTER ONE

There was a young woman sitting in the bar. Her name was Pearl. She was drinking gin and tonics and she held an infant in the crook of her right arm. The infant was two months old and his name was Sam.

The bar was not so bad. Normal-looking people sat around her eating pretzel logs. The management advertised it as being cool and it was. There was a polar bear of leaded glass hanging in the center of the window. Outside it was Florida. Across the street was a big white shopping center full of white sedans. The heavy white air hung visibly in layers. Pearl could see the layers very clearly. The middle layer was all dream and misunderstanding and responsibility. Things moved about at the top with a little more arrogance and zip but at the bottom was the ever-moving present. It was the present, it had been the present, and it was always going to be the present. Pearl was always conscious of this. It made her pretty passive and indecisive usually.

She was wearing an expensive dress although it was spotted and the wrong weight for the weather. She had no luggage but she had quite a bit of money. She had just come down from the North that morning and had been in the hotel just a little over an hour. She had rented a room here. The management had put a crib in the room for Sam. When they had asked her her name she had replied that it was Tuna, which was not true.

"Tuna," the management had said. "That is certainly an unusual name."

"Yes," Pearl said. "I've always hated it."

The hotel was close to the airport. Hundreds of hotels and apartments were close to the airport; nevertheless Pearl still felt that she was being obvious. She had never been in this city before but she felt that it was an obvious choice for a runaway. She would check out of the hotel tomorrow and go deeper into the city. Perhaps she would find a tourist home there. The home would have black shutters and a wrap-around porch. Pleasant, portly women would sit on the porch eating plates of key lime pie. She would become one of them. She would get old.

She felt Walker's gaze burning into her back. Walker's smart and silent gaze. Pearl's stomach trembled. She turned violently around and saw nothing. The baby woke with a muffled grunt.

Pearl ordered another gin and tonic. For some reason the waitress did not hear what she said.

"What?" the waitress said.

Pearl raised her glass. "A gin and tonic," she repeated.

"Certainly," the waitress said.

Pearl often mumbled and did not make herself clear. Frequently people believed her to be implying something with her words that she was not implying at all. Words, for her, were issued with stubborn inaccuracy. The children had told her once that the sun was called the sun because the real word for it was too terrible. Pearl felt that she knew all the terrible words but none of their substitutes. Substitutions were what made civilized conversation possible. Whenever Pearl attempted civilized conversation, it sounded like gibberish. She could never find the appropriate euphemisms. Death, Walker had said, is a euphemism. But after all, the knock on the door, the messenger, the awaited guest was not always death, was it?

Pearl thought so, probably, yes.

The waitress came back with Pearl's gin and tonic. She was a pretty girl with blond bobbed hair and a small silver cross around her neck. She bent down slightly to serve the drink. Pearl detected a faint odor of cat piss. This is not fair of me, Pearl thought kindly. Things in Florida sometimes presented the odor of cat piss. It was the vegetation.

"Why do you wear a cross?" Pearl asked.

The girl looked at her with faint disgust. "I like the shape," she said.

Pearl thought the remark to be a little crude. She sighed. She was becoming drunk. Her cheekbones reddened. The waitress went back to the bar and stood talking with a young man seated there. Pearl imagined them in some rank room after closing hours, spreading dough over their bodies and eating it off in some bourgeois rite. Pearl spread her hand and pressed her fingers hard against her cheekbones. She felt guilty and annoyed.

She also felt a little silly. She was running away from her home, from her husband. She had taken her little baby and carefully arranged a flight away in secret. She had boarded a plane and traveled twelve hundred miles in three hours. The deception that had been necessary! The organization! People were always talking to her at home, on her husband's island. She couldn't bear it any more. She had to have a new life.

Sometimes Pearl thought she really did not want to have a new life at all. She wanted to be dead. Pearl felt that dead people continue an existence not unlike the one suffered previously, but duller and less eventful and precarious. She had worked out this attitude about death after much thought but it didn't give her any comfort.

Pearl sipped her drink worriedly. Until recently, she had never drunk much. When she was fourteen, she'd had a drink, and in the last year she'd had maybe a dozen drinks in the whole year. When she was fourteen, she and a red-headed boy had drunk half of a fifth of gin in a broken-down bathhouse on a rainy summer day. She was wearing a cute checked bathing suit and a pullover sweater. On the wall of the bathhouse someone had carved the words NUT FLEA. After they had drunk the gin, the red-headed boy lay on top of her with all his clothes on. When she woke up, she was uncertain whether she had been introduced into sexuality or not. She walked briskly home and took a very hot bath. Nothing hurt. She kept running hot water over herself. She thought she was pregnant. When it became apparent that she was not pregnant, she feared that she was barren. She had been positive of this until recently. Now she realized she was not barren. Now she had this baby. Walker had given it to her.

She glanced at Sam once more. He seemed rudimentary but intense. He was a baby. He was her baby. Everyone said that he was perfect, and he was, in fact, a very nice baby. He had dark hair and a sweet little birthmark in the shape of a crescent moon to make him special. Shelly, after she had come back to the island with her own baby, had told Pearl that having a baby was like shitting a watermelon. Pearl would not have chosen that disgusting expression certainly, but she did feel that birthing was an extremely unnatural act. After she had passed Sam, she had gone blind for a day and a half. Her blindness hadn't brought darkness with it. No, her blindness had just taken away all the things she had become familiar with, the room she shared with Walker, the view of the meadow, the faces and the shapes of them there, and replaced them with unpleasant delusions.

She had imagined that the child had come stillborn, that it had awakened into life only through Walker's cry of rage. Walker was a persuasive, striking and imaginative man. Pearl could not dismiss the possibility that that he was capable of such a thing.

Pearl realized that she was no longer gazing at the baby on her hip, but at the back of the waitress' head instead. The waitress turned slowly toward Pearl. Pearl raised her arm. The waitress stared at her for a moment and then said something to the bartender. The bartender reached for a freshly washed glass and shook the droplets of water from it. He reached for the bottle of gin and poured.

Pearl dropped the hand that ordered the drink into a gesture for smoothing her hair.

Tomorrow she would have her hair cut and try to change her appearance. Tomorrow she would forget the past and think only of the future. Yesterday was part of the encircling never. Tomorrow was Halloween. She had seen it advertised at the airport. They were going to have a party for the elderly there. Tomorrow Pearl was going to make every effort to relegate the gigantic physical world to its proper position.

The waitress arrived with the gin and tonic and placed it beside the other one, which Pearl had hardly touched. Pearl began to drink them. Her gold wedding band clicked against the glass. The ring was part of the encircling never. She tried to work it off her finger but couldn't. The encircling never was the world that Walker's family possessed, the interior world she was leaving, the island home.

Outside, the sun continued to shine maniacally. Shouldn't it have set by now? Her hands trembled. Her hands were her ugliest feature. They were square and prematurely wrinkled. She stared at them and saw them curved around a comb, combing Walker's hair.

Walker would find her. She suddenly knew that. And if Walker didn't, Thomas surely would.

Thomas, her husband's brother. A man of the world. A man of extremes, of angers, ambitions. He and Walker looked very much alike. Their coloring and weight were the same. Their thick hair, their mouths ... The difference was, of course, that Pearl saw Walker with her heart. Once, however, Pearl had made a very embarrassing mistake. She had mistaken Thomas for Walker. It was shortly after she had come to the island, late one evening, on the landing outside their bedroom. His back was to her. He was facing the bookshelves. "Are you coming to bed soon?" she'd asked, touching his arm. Thomas turned and looked at her, his gaze flat and ironic, uncharged by love, and then had brushed past her, saying nothing. She had been grateful to him for ignoring the mistake but she had gone to her room, trembling, sweating with fear. And she had sat there, looking at objects in the room, not grasping their purpose or function anymore, very frightened, her desires and basic assumptions in doubt. Lamps, baskets, photographs, little jars of pills and scents. What were they for? What did the faces of things represent? What was it that she was supposed to recognize?

When the door to the bedroom had opened, later that night, Pearl had firmly shut her eyes.

She said, "Walker, I saw Thomas in the hallway tonight and I thought he was you."

The figure in the room approached and stood over her. Pearl had raised her hand and touched the chest's smooth skin.

Walker's voice had said, "The difference between Thomas and me is that he doesn't need women."

Walker's remark had not reassured Pearl as to the recognition of her desires. She didn't want to be needed by any of them. On the island there were a dozen children, more or less, and five adults. Thomas, Walker, Miriam and Shelly were family. Lincoln was Shelly's husband. He had been her teacher at college. From the way they told it, Shelly had kidnapped him.

Pearl supposed that she herself had been kidnapped as well. The family certainly did things in an unorthodox way. Shelly's baby was just a few days older than Sam. They'd named him Tracker, which seemed a pretty absurd name to Pearl, although she guessed that she had named him in some wacky way after Walker. Shelly had gone off to school and come back with a husband and a baby. Lincoln was a pompous fellow who sniffed excitedly when he thought he'd made a point in conversation. Lincoln's true predilections were uncertain, but he was nothing if not an adult. Pearl was never sure whether she should count herself among the children or the adults. The shirts or the skins. Wasn't that a phrase?

Pearl sipped her gin.

She spent most of her time with the children. They were always seeking her out and speaking outlandishly to her. Pearl felt that they had driven her to drink. But that was all right. They were just children. She was fond of them really. What had driven her away, what had made her feel that she couldn't bear it on the island for another day, was Thomas.

Pearl did not want her little Sam to be influenced by a man who could snap a child's mind as though it were a twig. She blamed Thomas for what had happened to Johnny. It didn't seem to occur to anyone else that Thomas was to blame, but it was very clear to Pearl. Johnny was a sensitive child and Thomas had pushed him too hard. Thomas thought Johnny was bright and he was determined to make him brighter. Johnny's loves were peaches, bottle rockets and sitting on a stool in the kitchen helping his mother, Miriam, make cakes. He had been a nice little boy, wistful and impressionable but with simple needs. He couldn't stand the weight of all that junk Thomas put into his head.

Johnny was six years old but the last time Pearl had gone into his room and looked at the bed, she hadn't seen a little boy of six at all, but a lump of white that looked like rising dough with a face tucked in it of the hundredth day of gestation.

The last time Pearl had gone into the room she had seen ants. There, in a committed procession, had come a hundred ants. Miriam had seen them too. Miriam had said that they shouldn't become alarmed. Had not ants come to Midas as a child and filled his mouth with grains of wheat? Had not insects visited Plato in his infancy, settling on his lips, ensuring him powerful speech? Pearl sweated. Pearl hadn't known what to say.

Johnny had started dying, or whatever it was analogous to

it, two months ago, in August. August was the month when Sam was born. August was also the month for the birthday party. The children had always celebrated their birthdays collectively. At the birthday party, Johnny had announced that he felt inhabited. He was inhabited by hundreds. There were cells in his body and all stronger than he. He couldn't keep them ordered. He couldn't keep them pleased. In the middle of the party Johnny had gone to his bed and hadn't gotten up from it since. He lay with his face in the pillow, his poor little body like a graveyard in which the family dead of several generations had been buried.

He had had beautiful eyes. Before he got his notions, he had been normal enough, gorging himself on chocolate rabbits at the appropriate time of year, learning how to sail and water-color and so on, and doing everything with those beautiful and command-ing eyes which were a luxurious violet color like certain depths of the sea.

In his illness, he said that he could see the blood moving though the veins of things. He said he thought he could induce the birds and the butterflies and animals of the picture books to come to life, to totter out of the books, leaving holes behind them. He said he was sure he could do this except he was afraid.

The child was overstimulated. He had been reading since the age of four. They *all* read at four. He worried about nuclear power and volcanoes and Beethoven's deafness. He worried about the people who wrote to Miriam and told her the terrible things that had happened to them. Thomas encouraged him in these worries because he thought they honed the mind. Thomas told Johnny he could do anything if he just set his mind to it. Wasn't Uri Geller able to make a closed rose unfurl just with the power of his thought? Hadn't Christ made a fig tree wither with just the power of his annoyance? Well, now Johnny was setting his mind to something analogous to dying, and Thomas was off ruining other babies' minds. Miriam had four-month-old twins, Ashbel and Franny, and Thomas was probably at them, even this very moment. Thomas loved babies. He would hold the twins and talk to them in French, in Latin. He would talk to them about Utrillo, about knights, about compasses. Thomas loved babies. He loved children. When they got to puberty he sent them off to boarding school and forgot about them.

In the bar, she took a breath of air, as though she were tasting freedom, and coughed slightly. She slipped her finger into Sam's small fist. She liked her baby. She was glad they were together, alone. She was glad that neither one of them would ever have to see Thomas again. She supposed, however, that the baby might grow to miss his cousins. And his father. Pearl herself would not miss Walker much. It was true that once Pearl had seen Walker with her heart but that was no longer so. Pearl didn't know Walker very well which was why she always set great store upon seeing him with her heart. He was very seldom on the island. She didn't know his business. She imagined that it simply might be taking women out to lunch and then sleeping with them. She had often wished, in the months when she was pregnant, that he would have been content enough to do just that with her, instead of bringing her back to his family and marrying her.

That seemed unnecessary.

He could still have given her her baby but she would not have had to spend that lonely year on the island where she was the only one, it seemed, with any ordinary sense at all.

She was going to keep Sam calm and common. She would not let him play in a questionable manner. Everything would be bought in a store and have some sort of a guarantee. When he got sick, she was going to call a doctor.

Even when Johnny weighed only eighteen pounds, Thomas had not called a doctor. He had brought over a psychiatrist. It was like contacting a voodoo priest, Pearl thought. The psychiatrist had come over to the island in a velour jogging suit and had spoken at length about love, rage and the triumph of hateful failure. The psychiatrist had suggested that Johnny was a very willful, angry, even dangerous little boy.

Miriam had cried. They all realized that Johnny was willful. He had always gotten everything he wanted, usually just by the demands of his beautiful, insistent eyes. But it didn't seem so bad. It didn't bring anybody any harm. As for the idea that Johnny was angry and cruel, how could anyone, least of all Miriam, believe that? Miriam could only remember him as the child who fell asleep on her white bed after a day in the sun, smelling wonderful, tiny sea shells stuck to his bottom.

A tear popped up in Pearl's eye as she thought of Miriam, crying. Poor Miriam. She could see her sitting by Johnny's bed, trying to talk to him, trying to bring him back, away from the dark child's path.

Poor Miriam. She told Pearl that she would sit in Johnny's room and see all the confusions in poor Johnny's head. There was a smell of sex and death and cooking, Miriam said. The slap of bodies coupling and quarreling was terrific. The racket of baroque construction. The cries and slithering, the giggles and complaints. The babies and fabulous animals. The old men. It was dark in Johnny's room, but the people in his head were beautiful luminous clouds, delineated by flowing golden lines. The darkness, Miriam said to Pearl, held only the path. The children's path. Dark.

Pearl put a pretzel log in her mouth. It tasted as though she were eating her napkin. Miriam made wonderful pretzels. Pearl might never get a decent pretzel again. Miriam was the best cook Pearl had ever known. She loved to bake and make. If it weren't for her, everyone was well aware, the children would live on nothing but honeysuckle and berries. She loved cooking. She never wearied of it. The gathering, the selecting. The boning, chopping, grating. The only day she ever made a mistake in the kitchen was the day her husband, Les, had abandoned her, a week before the twins were born. She'd put sugar instead of salt in the béchamel.

Les had been a mess. He'd been the gardener. They'd found him when the family had vacationed once in Sea Island, Georgia, in the days before Thomas decided they shouldn't vacation. Les was a borderline simpleton with a big handsome face and a large appetite. Miriam had never paid much attention to him. She was too busy with her sewing, cooking, shopping. How Miriam loved to shop! She approached supermarkets with joyously clenched teeth. Pearl had never done well in supermarkets. She saw Miriam as a successful conqueror penetrating a hostile country, routing out the perfect endive, the blemishless peach, the excellent cheese ... Miriam had confided to Pearl once that she was glad Les was gone. Miriam had told Pearl he had a business bright and shiny as a carrot.

Pearl looked at the rings of moisture her glass had made on the barroom table. She rearranged Sam in her arms. There was a crack in the formica that had hair in it. Pearl put her cocktail napkin over it. On the napkin were animals drinking and playing poker. Pearl put her hand over the cocktail napkin.

On the wall in Johnny's room was a picture Thomas had given him. It was a face made up from the heads and parts of animals. Arcimboldo. All the children thought it terribly witty. They envied Johnny for having it. Johnny adored Thomas for having given it to him. Pearl had never thought it very witty. She found it disgusting. A picture razored from an art book. Antlers, ears tusks, haunches, tails, teeth ... making up the head of a man. The man's bulbous nose a rabbit's haunches, his hair a tangle of wildcats and horses, his eye a wolf's open mouth. No wonder Johnny had nightmares, that wretched thing being the last he saw before he fell asleep at night. The head's adam's apple, a bull's balls ... Well, that was rather witty, Pearl thought.

Poor Johnny. Pearl could not remember what he looked like. Sometimes her memory was not good at all. Pearl would be the first to admit that her mind was like a thin pool, on the bottom of which lay huge leaves, slowly softening. Or had Thomas said that to her once? Rudely.

She remembered enough, actually. More than she cared to. She remembered the way the psychiatrist had stood in the living room, while Miriam wrung her hands, and said, "Your child dreads to become alive and real because he fears that in doing so, the risk of annihilation is immediately potentiated."

She remembered Miriam confessing to her once that she had taken to spanking Johnny. She did it tentatively, for it felt so queer, and then stopped almost immediately and began to rock him. His pale bones floated beneath her anxious hands. She cradled him in her arms and pressed her face into his hot tangled hair. Everything felt wrong. She combed out his hair with her own hairbrush, hoping it would order his thoughts. She put a little copper bell on the table beside his bed so that he could call for her should he want her, should he ever change his mind. Pearl remembered Miriam's hopeless voice drifting out of his room:

"Mommy's leaving now, but in the morning I'll make you french toast. You can put up the flag. You can go quahoging with the boys . . ."

Never again would Miriam see the tiny sea shells on Johnny's bottom. Never again would he come back as he had been. Never, never, never. You cannot keep things the way they are. They go away. They change. There has never been an exception to this rule. No mercy has ever been shown.

Oh to bring back the days when stars spoke at the mouths of caves.

To go back to those times when one could not know, for the darkness, in what ways they had lost their former selves . . .

Pearl was beginning to feel a little nauseated. On the plane, she had won a bottle of champagne by being the passenger who, in a contest over Richmond, had come closest to guessing the combined ages of the flight crew, a number which she could not now recall. She had drunk the champagne all by herself.

The drinks here didn't taste as good as the ones she made herself on the island. It was the sulphur in the ice cubes here or something.

A well-dressed woman with terrible breath came up to her table and bent down over Sam. She jiggled a swizzle stick at him. She thought he was wonderful.

"What all flavor is that little thing?" she asked Pearl. "Chocolate or vanilla?"

Blankly, Pearl looked at Sam and then at the woman.

"It's just an old country expression," the woman said, "to mean boy or girl?"

"Oh," Pearl said. People are nice here, she thought. Sam jumped in her lap. Pearl closed her eyes, and finished her drink.

When she opened them again, the woman was gone. Across the room behind a phalanx of bottles was a mirror. Pearl did not look good in it. In the mirror, a couple appeared to be sitting beside her with a small alligator on the table between them. When Pearl turned and saw the actual table, she saw that it was so. The alligator was of the size one usually finds deceased in southern gift shops, next to the kumquat jellies. This one was dully alive. Its small feet made a gently, rustling sound, like leaves.

"You're just too much, Earl," the woman said.

"It's got a dong in it big as its whole self, you know that?" Earl said. "Goddamnedest thing."

Pearl firmly signed her check with her room number. She got up and began walking out of the bar. Her legs felt as though they were wrapped in mattresses.

The bartender interrupted her careful progress. "Ma'am," he said. "There's a call for you." Unsurprised, she took the phone, and shifting Sam to her other arm, put the receiver to her ear.

There was nothing. A fading singing. Like a child's nonsense rhymes. Or perhaps it was a problem in her inner ear.

She put the receiver back on the hook and went into the lobby. She took the elevator up to the fifth floor. She walked down a long corridor. There was a maid there, pushing a cart, collecting supper trays that guests had left outside their doors. The maid had a piece of cheese in her mouth.

Pearl fumbled a moment with the lock to her room, then pushed the door open. The room was cool and cramped. Someone had wheeled a crib into the room. There was a crib and a bed and a chair.

Walker sat in a chair, facing her.

"Hello," he said. He got up and touched her face with his fingers. "Darling," he said.

CHAPTER TWO

The first time Pearl had ever seen Walker, she had been shoplifting in a department store. Walker had seen her in the act of committing crimes and he had taken her off with him. This was the way it happened one year ago. Even when she tried to remember meeting him another, more respectable way, she couldn't, because that was the way it had happened.

Pearl had had several hundred dollars worth of stuff jammed in her shoulder bag. She had been going up and down the escalators, a bored pretty girl with freckles. A delightful girl wearing a paisley dress with a little round collar. At that time, she had been married for six days to a young man named Gene Jones. In her bag she had fancy jams and jewelry, sweaters and books and an espresso coffeepot. She did not know how to make espresso and Gene did not like coffee. It made him go to the bathroom and Gene did not like the bathroom, which Pearl did not keep very clean. Gene drank only apple juice. He was a level-headed young man, determined to win a school board seat in an upcoming election and thereby launch himself into politics. Now he was just a gym teacher but soon he would be a state representative. It was just a matter of time. But at the time of their marriage, he was just a gym teacher and smooth all over from the many showers he took. His hair was always damp. He chewed sugarless gum and could draw in his belly so tight that there was just about two inches of him between his belly button and tail bone. When he took her to bed he had a gymnast's routine and timing. He performed as though clocked. They made love four or five times a day and he managed to utilize all the positions he knew each time. There was a pace to their love-making that made Pearl feel healthy and calm. Nevertheless, the unsubtle sex between them soon became tediously balanced between the childish and the corrupt. When she was not in bed with Gene making her graceful and studied offerings, she did not like him much. They lived in a small hot house on a sand alley. Outside there were rats and birds. There was one very ill, slow rat that had wandered around outside the house for all the six days that she and Gene had been married. Pearl would shout at it through the screen. It appeared about the same time every morning and would walk wretchedly back and forth in the short grass. It was really not an unpleasant-looking rat—that is, it did not have sores or patchy fur. She really didn't mind it much. She pitied it for whatever gruesome end was waiting for it.

The house came furnished. The woman who owned the house would come over every day and chat with Pearl. She would tell her about her husband. Her husband's name was Arthur and he was fifty-five. "Just the age when most men start to slow down," the woman would tell Pearl. "But Arthur is still going strong." The woman told Pearl that her husband got especially aroused right after he sprayed their property for bugs. "I noticed it last year," she said. "We had ants and roaches and right after Arthur sprayed he would start to look for me. He would get so passionate that he didn't care if I did my housework or even cook. Last year was bad enough, but this year it's worse. On weekends he sprays sometimes two and three times a day. It's really getting me down." Pearl felt sorry for her landlady. "I'm so tired," the woman would tell Pearl.

Gene and Pearl didn't have anything of their own except a television set. Television light was marvelous to fuck by, Gene always said. Pearl tried to imagine buying a lot of things and having a lot of possessions but she didn't quite know what these possessions would be. She had never collected things, even as a child. Buying and having things seemed to be a way of knowing who one was. One was an aggregate of interests and desires. People received energy and solace from wanting things and then getting them. Pearl wanted energy and solace. She felt that if she could only get interested in and knowledgeable about a kinky subject, for example hockey or sharks, she would be a more contented person. She could not just be fucking all the time. Soon something more would have to happen. Pearl did not feel that she was a real person. She felt that she deceived Gene terribly.

The fifth day of their marriage fell on a Sunday and they spent all day in bed. Pearl had plumped some pillows behind her back and was gazing at Gene's sweaty, quivering shoulders. She felt that imagination was not what it was cracked up to be. She felt that innovation was impossible, for was there not always the ambiguous memory of any act? She patted his shoulder comfortingly. He was just like anybody else after all. He did his best. She could not stop patting his shoulder. Finally he stopped and rolled over. Pearl went into the kitchen and boiled some water for tea. She was twenty years old and didn't know anybody. Her parents were dead. The only relative she had was an elderly aunt who had been living in the Polynesian Village Hotel somewhere in Arizona for two years. It was expensive, she wrote to Pearl, but she loved it. Outside her window was a hedge pruned into the shape of the Polynesian God of Happiness. The place was highly organized and much more comprehensive than life. The aunt sent Pearl recipes.

"Oh," Pearl said aloud. She did not want any more recipes. She returned to the bedroom and looked at Gene for a long time. He was sleeping in the white Magnavox light. Couldn't one get cancer from television?

"Ohhh," she said again, a sound more like the sound of love than any she had been able to muster. He was so substantial lying there. Would there be no end to it? She felt ghostly with her solitude. The hedges outside her window were in the shape of dying hedges. It was a woman, it must have been, back in the beginning of things who decided that death should be a part of life. A man wouldn't have thought of it. Women chose death so that they would always feel sorry.

Gene's eyes wandered open. "My beloved," he said thickly at her and then fell asleep again.

The next morning, Pearl decided to go to the store. She wanted to do something she had never done before and in that way discover something about herself. She felt that her real self was walking in a sisterly manner beside her, holding her hand but otherwise not being very instructive. She stole the shoulder bag first. She put her own plastic navy-colored purse on the floor and shoved it most of the way under a counter with her foot. Her purse held her driver's license and six little sugared doughnuts on a card that she had bought from a machine that morning in a gas station. It also had her wallet with ten dollars in it. She took the money out and put it in her new bag. As she walked down the aisles she tore the tags off the bag with her thumbnail and let them drop to the floor. No one touched her shoulder. No one told her to come with them. She went upstairs and down, taking things. It was so easy to have things! She felt a little better.

It was almost lunchtime when she met Walker. She had been trying to decide whether she should go up to the top floor of the department store to a rotating restaurant and have an iced tea and a salad. That was what women did, wasn't it? While she was trying to decide this she palmed some bracelets off a counter and slipped them on her wrist.

Walker said to her, "You're going to get caught. I've caught you."

Pearl stood very still. Her backbone was hot, burning through her dress. She felt as though someone had set a match to it. Pearl stood very still but she felt that her head was rotating wildly. Once, on the soundless television, she saw a baseball player beaned by a ball. His fractured head began swinging crazily, in all sorts of impossible positions. He'd looked as though he cared so much, he was doing it all so hard. His head was making up for the years of stillness ahead.

Pearl brought her hand up slowly to her head. It was still. The fear she felt had nothing to do with the situation of being arrested for common shoplifting. That would simply be an embarrassment. She would feel like a fool. She would be fingerprinted; she would be put in a cell and given a sandwich and then Gene would be notified and he would come and get her and he would be terribly embarrassed too. He would pay something to get her out. They would get in the car together and drive home. He would pat her hand. He would not mention the incident again.

This had nothing to do with the anxiousness Pearl felt at the sound of Walker's voice. This applied only to the rules of a benign and banal world she had just fallen from. The other, the fear, the loss of herself beside him, was nameless and complete.

She turned to the man standing beside her. He had dark hair and eyes. Smooth, marvelous skin. His hands rested on her shoulder. He was a large man. Even his hair seemed weighty. She knew he was not going to arrest her. His authority had nothing to do with the law. His hands on her were a hunter's hands, dressing her down. She felt stretched, spread, terribly exposed.

"Come on now," he said. "Come with me."

She felt as though he were emptying her, right there on the spot, absorbing little parts of her, nullifying them, closing the little exits in her mind. Jesus walked out. The doors kept shutting in her mind. She did not want to interfere. Windows shut. Her heart was in twilight. She was nothing, in a field, children running across her heart. She was nothing, nowhere, with this man. A strange thought crept across her mind. Once there were four animals who supported the world in the sky. Then one of them was killed. This could never be redeemed. This could never be atoned for. Pearl felt so lonely and sad. The animal died. Things could never be all right. Pearl had never felt such loneliness or been filled with such longing.

She put the handbag that wasn't her own down on the floor. And then she followed this man who was Walker. They passed through the store and into the street. They were in his car, traveling out of the city. As they drove, he questioned her politely, about her past, her associations and arrangements. She answered, she knew. She heard her voice, replying, wrapping up her life for him. It had a beginning and an end. He listened attentively. The two of them, she recounting, he listening, disposed of it. It was their first act together.

He pulled into a motel on the highway, one of a large, popular chain. She knew of course that he would do this and she felt that this was somehow to her advantage, this presumption, this knowledge. This is how it all begins. It was the hereditary flow of women to have such helpless understanding. The wound that opened again and again. The wound that was never fatal. She felt better. That was all there was to it, even with this man. She was not lost, nor had she been found. She was not doing anything particularly abnormal. She was in an efficiently run motel. There would be children in the swimming pool with styrofoam bubbles on their backs. There would be a loop of paper on the toilet seat to show that it had been cleaned. There would be a grip cemented on the shower wall. There would be no danger here.

Pearl walked into the lobby with Walker as he registered.

"What do you drink?" he asked, writing on the form, "Thomas. *Mr. and Mrs. Walker Thomas.*"

"I don't know," she said. She didn't know about drinking. She hadn't had a drink since the red-headed boy in the bathhouse.

Walker's hand on her neck was soft. His touch was gentle, pitiless, and again she felt the dread of nothingness, the extinguishment of light. She did not want to be responsible for maintaining the light in herself. She sagged against him slightly and then straightened.

He guided her out of the lobby and into the adjacent bar. The only people there were a woman bartender and an overweight couple drinking Cokes.

"Kids are wonderful," the man was saying. "Our four-year-old, the things he says! The other night he wouldn't go to sleep, you know. He was making a little fuss and saying he was afraid of the dark and all and mother here says to him, 'Don't be afraid of the dark. God's in the room with you,' and he says, 'I know God's here but I want somebody with *skin* on.'"

The woman started to laugh. She was plump and blond and smelled like a rising cake.

"Isn't that a kid though," the bartender said.

Pearl put her hand out and held on to the bar. She thought that this was the most horrible story she had ever heard in her life.

Walker bought a fifth of bourbon and they walked out of the bar and down a concrete walkway to the last room in the complex. On the grass rimming the walkway were many arrangements of pets' feces.

Walker unlocked the door. The room was cold and dark. She started to undress immediately. Walker sat on the bed and smoked a cigarette. She knew it would be like this, that he would sit and smoke and watch her. The bottoms of her feet were dirty. It came from wearing sandals all the time. She rubbed her bare feet awkwardly on the carpet.

"I'm getting fat," she said. Actually she was thin. But she knew she would say that.

Walker said nothing. His eyes were hooded, secret. There seemed to be no white to them in the dimness of the room. He put two pillows behind his head and stretched out full length on the bed. She lay down beside him. The way he lay beside her so heavily, so powerfully at rest, excited her. Her own body was unable to accept this force, this stillness in him. She caressed him. The cloth of his suit was expensive. She was sweating, burning with her chastity beside him. She could not look at his face. She began undressing him, stealthily, a sexual robber. A gangster already caught and sentenced. He stopped her.

"Wait," he said, "it's all right. Tell me something, anything. Start anywhere."

Pearl returned to herself again though not as successfully as before. She shook her head dully. She sat up. She was twenty years old, her nipples were like the hard tight buds of a new tree. She had been married but now it seems she is not married. She does not have her pocketbook. She does not have any identification.

"I had a dog once," she said. "My father shot it. My mother and father told me that the dog had attacked a little girl, another little girl, and ripped her arm, and that my father had to shoot it."

Pearl looked at Walker. Such a nice dog he had been. A black shepherd with brandy-colored paws. She had never seen him bite any little girl.

"I never learned how to row a boat. I never learned how to push my sunglasses up on the crown of my head like the other girls."

Walker said nothing.

"I never learned how to masturbate," Pearl said. "There was not much that I learned actually but I've never understood why I do not know how to masturbate."

"You were all alone. You could not imagine the lover."

"My stomach bloated. I grew rigid. I took myself carefully, moment by moment…"

"And then nothing?"

"Soon I became embarrassed."

"You could not imagine the lover. But I'm your lover now."

"Yes," she said. It had been very dark in the room, that first room with Walker. Outside it was night. The air conditioner obliterated any of the noise that might have been out there. He had not touched her since they had entered the room. He was still facing her. She was still. But it was as though her life had finally been put into motion by this man.

"Why were you in the department store?" Pearl asked. "Why am I with you now? I didn't have to follow you. I shouldn't have to be with you."

She wondered if she was going to be murdered and have her name in all the papers like her father, who had murdered himself.

"You're like a pretty piece of glass on the beach, a piece of driftwood. Something waiting to be found, something waiting for someone like me to discover its personality. You've been washed up by the tide. I've collected you." His voice was smooth, striped with sun in the darkness like the moving flanks of an animal. "You can think of it like that, if you wish," he said.

"I won't think about it," she said. She was very tired. She fell asleep. When she awoke she was on her stomach. She felt as though she were being breathed on by something. It was not her own breath. She was the breath, rolling in meaty jaws. She flung her arm behind her and grasped the thick hair of his head, which was dry and fragrant. She writhed in the darkness with him, unprotesting. She started to moan. It was like singing. She could not stop. He rose and turned her beneath him. She was so light, just a feather, just a bone. He fell into her again. Her breasts entered his mouth. He was a tree, she a snake, coiling about him. She was many snakes coiling in the sunshine by the tree's roots, upon the ground, everywhere.

He let her slide to the floor. She raised her haunches to him, she pressed her cheek to the carpet. Dust in her nostrils, the color of the carpet, a rose shade. A pattern that swirled inward, into the buds of flowers. He fixed his mouth against her neck and came into her with a low growl. She was not with him, but she felt a keen and startling pleasure. And she went with that, kept going with that, until she was far away.

Hours later, Pearl had been almost surprised to wake into an ordinary morning. She peered through the blinds and could see travelers packing their cars. An irritated mother was hitting a child on the shoulders with the child's own Barbie and Ken lunch box. Engines were starting. A bathtub was draining in the room beside her. It reminded her that she should take a bath.

She bathed quickly and dressed, then unlocked the door to the outside. Walker lay on the bed, on his back, watching her with his dark eyes.

"I have to get a few things," she said.

"Put it on the bill," he said. "Or take money if you'd rather. My wallet's in my jacket there."

She took a few dollars from his wallet.

"Don't disappear now," he said.

"Oh no," she said. The thought hadn't occurred to her.

He smiled. "We're going to my home," he said simply. As simply as that. "We have to drive about twenty miles to the ferry, and then it's forty minutes by steamer to Saddleback Island. Then we take a boat over to our island. It's seven miles, a little over half an hour if Joe has the Chris-Craft there. We'll leave as soon as you get back."

"I didn't know there were any islands beyond Saddleback," Pearl said.

Walker swung his legs over the side of the bed. "A few little ones. Ours is the largest. Twenty thousand acres. We've owned it for one hundred years."

"Oh," Pearl said. "I just didn't know there were other islands there." She felt stupid. She averted her eyes from his as she stood up.

"There's no reason for anyone to know about them," he said, then laughed. "The state knows we're there, though. They just raised our taxes last year from six to forty thousand."

"Oh," she said. "Well, I'll just get a few things." She gestured toward the door.

He was dressed and waiting for her when she returned to the room. They drove mostly in silence. It was early autumn and the day was cool. Pearl had known about Saddleback for years. It was an elegant resort island. They called the fine old homes "cottages" there. They called the simpler but comfortable houses "shacks." As a teen-ager, Pearl felt that if she could only have a safari-cloth skirt and a cranberry-colored sweater and walk those streets of summer with their expensive crowds, her life would turn out all right.

Not once on their drive to the steamer had she thought of Gene or of those dead nights. She had been taken away as though by drowning. They would never find her living face again. No announcement would arrive.

Once she said to Walker, "Will we be together now? From now on?"

He shrugged.

"If we don't have the time, we'll have eternity," she said, half laughing, not really knowing what she meant.

"You know about that eternity," he said. "There's a rock that's a hundred miles high and a hundred miles wide. Once every thousand years a little bird comes to this rock to sharpen its beak."

"I'm not a child," Pearl said.

He smiled. They passed a sign advertising a palmist. A gigantic hand. MADAME CLAVELL. The hand was covered with starbursts of light. The little lights were .22 holes. Flattened in the center of the palm were the remnants of something feathered.

Pearl opened her mouth and then shut it again.

"So much even for the little bird," Walker said.

Pearl laughed. She felt that she owed this man a good deal. He had awakened her, not to life, but to some sweet void in which she felt she could dwell forever. But she was so tired. Her body, slumped against the blond leather of the car seats, was a weight too heavy to be borne. Her exhaustion was strange to her. She closed her eyes and fell into dreams.

She was having a baby in a large, freshly cut field. There was blood on the grass but it may not have been her own. It was cold but dry. It might have been color, not blood at all, an ivy winding through the grass. Her thighs were spread. Her arms were spread. She was going to have a baby. She knew that those around her were going to cut open her stomach and fold back the flaps of skin and unfold the baby from her like a bridal gown. She knew that they would abandon her there, her terrible dark wound a nest for the flying creatures of the night.

The baby slid out of her. It was beautiful, black and silver, heaving for breath, glossy with her blood and water. She could not see him clearly enough. She strained to see him. They assured her that he was beautiful. She tossed her head fretfully from side to side. She wanted to feed him. She wanted to see him so that she could begin to love. She was afraid she didn't know anything about love. That love was like physics, something that somebody had tried to teach her about once, something she had not caught onto. The figures that had been on the rim of the meadow now surrounded her. They assured her that he was perfect. And the fact that he had been born at dusk was propitious, they said. For that was the luckiest hour.

Their voices were low, peaceful. She couldn't understand why she know what they were saying. It was not words they were saying. It was a dream, she knew. If she could relax in her dream, she would wake up. But it made her fret. She was in a car traveling. This is how people dreamed. She was awake now but she kept her eyes clenched tight.

In her dream it had become too dark for Pearl to see her baby.

She opened her eyes. "I can't," she said.

"We're almost at the boat," he said. "Then we'll be home."

"I'm married," she said awkwardly.

"That was nothing. Six days. No one's married for six days." He passed his hand over her hair. "Little Mouse."

"Oh," she said.

"Little mouse," he repeated. "Little lost soul."

She looked at him, her eyes widening. What is the redeeming question? she thought. I have failed to ask the redeeming question and now it is too late.

"You're with me," he said.

CHAPTER THREE

They had taken the steamer over to Saddleback. They stood on the deck with the other travelers. Everyone was tanned and there were many bicycles and dogs.

A woman said to her friend, "They bought a rocking horse that had documents with it, proof that it had belonged to Rommel. It cost them a fortune and they gave it to Jennifer, can you imagine . . ."

Beside Pearl was a man in a clerical collar, wearing a seersucker suit and sneakers and taking pictures with a Nikon. He had a dog leashed to the railing and occasionally, turning away from the view, which was pretty much blue and empty, he would take pictures of the dog.

Pearl would grab plastic cups that were rolling around the deck and put them in the trash. A man wearing dyed blue Jockey shorts and Mexican sandals said, "I've taught him how to fuck and play tennis and still he won't marry me."

The boat rolled across the simple sea and made Pearl a little queasy.

When it docked, everyone waited on the narrow stairs. The man in the Jockey shorts said to the man of the collar, "I have a sister, Father, who is a real meatball. She goes into the nunnery and the first thing you know she's pregnant and she tells me, she says, 'Jesus thought of me.' That's how she said it happened, I swear. What do you think of that, Father?"

Everyone trooped to the hold and squeezed into their cars, which were parked very close together. There was a convertible parked next to Walker's Mercedes. It had a cat carrier in it. A rounded gray paw extended limply. A woman was screaming at her husband about it. She would look unhappily into the box and then scream at her husband. Her husband looked embarrassed.

Walker drove swiftly across the island toward Morgansport. They passed through several pretty villages, old whaling ports with healthy vistas, with streets lined with elm trees that had escaped disease. Pearl wanted to linger there. She wanted Walker to show her the sights, but he was uninterested in Saddleback Island. His island, their island, lay beyond.

Walker garaged the car on the lane that led to their private pier. There was a long barn on one side of the lane for the family's cars. The walls of the barn were papered with posters. One of the posters advertised a circus. It showed the face of a clown. One half of the clown's face was made up very sadly, the other half leered in delight.

"I love clowns," Pearl said to Walker. "They're like children. They can do anything. They can get away with anything."

"You admire children, do you?" Walker asked.

"I don't know, I've never known any really. I was talking about clowns."

Posters were plastered upon posters. She saw the rump of a dappled horse halved by a ring of fire.

Even then, the thought of having children had depressed her and she sighed. "I suppose you will want us to have a child together, won't you?" she said.

Walker put his arm around her. He had looked like a businessman, slightly out of place in his fawn-colored suit, an oversized man, but easeful as he walked, his arm lightly and possessively encircling Pearl's waist.

An old, highly varnished motor launch was tied up to the dock.

There was a figure in white slouched in the launch. The figure was a boy, dressed in rumpled white pants and a shirt. His hair was white. His eyebrows were thick and white. He was chewing gum and smiling at Pearl in a way she simply hadn't the means to interpret. Pearl never forgot her bewilderment at the sight of him.

"This is my nephew, Joe," said Walker. "Joe is nine. He tries to make a point of never speaking to adults."

The boy helped them aboard. He started the engine and then sat in the stern in an elaborate wicker chair. He tipped the chair backward on two legs and steered with one hand while he held the other hand to his tanned cheek. The white light of the water danced in his eyes.

Pearl could not believe that Joe was only nine. He appeared almost twice that age, as though his efforts at remaining a child had prematurely aged him. Pearl had difficulty in not staring at his obvious erection. Joe seemed unaware of it himself. Children that age couldn't have erections like that anyway, could they? Perhaps he was just fooling around. Perhaps it was a prop, like they used in the old morality plays.

The child said nothing. He concentrated upon chewing his gum as though it were his jaws that were powering the boat.

It was cold, and Joe gave Pearl an orange windbreaker. She was very cold. She had no sense of anticipation. She could not imagine what it would be like there. She had never had much curiosity about things. She regarded this in a way like a gift, like a talent conferred. It had kept her from disappointment, even from sorrow.

She saw a sliver of moon in the green sky, like a sunrise. She crept beneath Walker's arm and watched in safety, like an arboreal creature in a midnight nest. As they headed out, the sky turned slowly gray, a creamy silver like the inside of a sea shell. A solitary cormorant flew past them, very close, the color of iron in the fog. Time passed. She felt warmer. The day was utterly without color or warmth, but she began to feel comfortable. She felt oddly illuminated, transilluminated, as though the sun had found a place within her on this journey, yet even as she felt this, the sun turned into something else, quite simple, the knowledge that she could never again be what she had been once.

The fog lifted in patches, became clouds. On either side of them, she saw the island, green and still. It had taken them almost an hour. Seven miles. It might have been seven years. She supposed it wouldn't seem so long in the future.

Joe brought the launch up to within several hundred yards of the shore and then proceeded with some deft, complex maneuvers through rocks into a small cove. It was almost high tide. The rocks were invisible from a distance, but looking over the varnished railings into the water, she could see their messy, jagged tops slide by.

"What's the name of your island?" Pearl asked Walker.

"We never named it," he said, turning from her for a moment while he lit a cigarette. "On the maps it's called 'Hart Island' and you'll hear some people in Morgansport refer to it like that, but that has nothing to do with us. They call it that not because of any Revolutionary War type deer tale, but because, I think, the island resembles a heart. From the air, at any rate." He laughed. "You could say that the house was on the left ventricle."

Joe cut the engines and brought the boat up quietly to the dock. The land was absolutely still, and Pearl saw nothing, not even a bird. There were several other vessels tied up to the dock, in all manner of sleekness or disrepair. The tide was still coming in. A brisk wind carried it with a slap against the pilings. Walker helped her out and then helped Joe tie the lines. There was an old Buick parked nearby on the dark, hard sand. They got into it.

"No showing off now, Joe," Walker said.

Pearl and Walker sat in the back of the Buick. The interior was mildewed and there were deep tears in the upholstery. Pearl looked at the boy's neck as they drove. His profile was flat, averted.

His long white hair swirled around his face in the wind. It could have been an old woman driving them. But then her eyes met his in the mirror and they were the eyes of a stern, precocious child. Walker told her that Joe had refashioned the old car himself so that he would be able to drive it. The boy loved to do anything with machines. When he was four, he had been convinced that his real father was an astronaut and he had built a space vehicle for himself which he had then attempted to fly from the roof, breaking his leg in the process.

Pearl looked amazed at the boy's smug and reckless profile.

"Goodness," she said.

They drove for long minutes down a road that was little more than a sandy track. She saw other roads branching off and disappearing into tangle. Some of the land had been cleared for pasturage but there were no animals visible. There were a few small wooden pens collapsing into the overgrowth.

"Do you raise animals here?" she asked.

"No, that's from Grandfather Aaron's day. Great-grandfather Aaron, really. He made his fortune from animals, one way or another. The children will tell you all about him. They're fascinated by him. I see him as a simple butcher myself. But a lucky man with money."

The Buick lurched past a marsh and there was a glimpse of the sea. Among the cattails and spartine grass of the rich, organic shore was a lone tree. High in its branches was a collection of boards, a playhouse.

"Oh," Pearl exclaimed. "I used to have one of those. It's nice here, isn't it? Islands are nice. They're a whole other world. I like it." She lowered her voice so Joe couldn't hear. "I like it your loving me and bringing me here."

The branches of trees crackled and pounded against the car's sides. From a distance, Pearl heard the sympathetic lament of church bells.

"Now don't tell me you have your own chapel on this island too?" she said, feeling lighthearted. "The mainland God isn't good enough for the Thomases?"

"That's just the children playing with the bell on the house," Walker said.

Then Joe had taken a sharp corner and the house was before them. The wheels spun in the sand and Pearl's head was lightly thrown back by the jolt. The sky was blue, a living seething blue. It charged her with energy, memory, a kind of competence. The memory had resulted not from any experience she could recall. It was rather almost chemical, something innate. A memory without an error.

The car stopped. "Here we are then," Walker said to Pearl. To the boy, he said, "You can't drive nails, Joe."

Joe shrugged and yawned, exposing the enormous wad of gum in his mouth. Pearl realized that she was sweating. Joe seemed to be looking at her without focusing on her. His eyes were alert and engaging but they just were not looking at anything. Pearl was relieved when he suddenly turned and ran off to join another boy who was just emerging from the house. The boy's head seemed covered with feathers.

At the time, the house had seemed more or less familiar to Pearl. Like a seasonal hotel. One to which she had never been taken before, certainly, but recognizable all the same. A rambling three-storied structure with a tightly shingled roof. Several of the rooms had little balconies on which were tattered canvas chairs. The house seemed to have been built at various times with a changing vision, but with all its styles it maintained the carelessness and simplicity that the rich sometimes bestow on their homes. The windows were paned with old thick glass and buckled out slightly. The wood was warm and smooth like skin. There were baroque and fanciful embellishments here and there. On the roof was a weather vane of a man shooting a wolf. Separating the first floor from the second was a band of lighter colored, much-embellished wood. Gamboling *putti* it seemed to Pearl, although she really couldn't make it out. Wrapped around the house was a wide porch upon which half a dozen children were playing. Some of them didn't have a stitch on.

"Walker, Walker," they cried out happily. For an instant, his name was the only utterance in the bawling Pearl recognized. Then a tiny girl touched Pearl's arm and lisped, "I swallowed my tooth but the Tooth Fairy gave me a quarter anyway."

The girl patted Pearl's dress. "Do you have anything pretty you'd like to give me?" she asked.

"Don't be impolite, Sweet," Walker said. "This is Pearl. Trip, Peter, Johnny, this is Pearl."

The children looked at her with mock gravity.

"Hello, Pearl," they said softly.

Walker opened the door. "I want to show you our rooms," he said.

They stepped into a long, wide hallway with a staircase rising at the end.

"Over here is the library," Walker said. "We'll come down here for cocktails later."

Pearl looked in and saw a large fireplace with a heavy oak mantel, a scattering of comfortable chairs and red and pink rugs. In the corner two boys were playing a board game. They did not look up.

From the other side of the hall Pearl smelled bread and could hear a woman singing softly. She followed Walker toward the stairs. The house was warm, almost airless. Even inside, the wood had a smooth velvety look, the wide floor boards almost white with age and scrubbing. Some of the children's drawings had been framed and hung on the wall, mixed in with two Picasso oils, a Sargent water color, and several Blake drawings.

"Are those real?" Pearl asked, squinting.

"The Blakes are copies," Walker said.

Christ was blessing little children. Good and bad angels were struggling for a baby.

The second floor was brighter. It had a slightly gamy smell. The rooms they passed were definitely the warrens of children. Walker told her that many of the children here were the family's by adoption. His brother, Thomas, was very fond of children. For years he had gathered them, all manner of misfits and foundlings who were raised in a long and indulged childhood with every possible freedom. Thomas encouraged their fantasies. Thomas gave them social graces and intellectual hungers. Thomas had enough money to do as he wished and what he wished was to educate children according to his interests.

"What are Thomas' interests?" Pearl asked.

They had climbed another flight of stairs. Pear was quite out of breath. She licked her lips still salty from the boat ride. Up above her was a skylight which disclosed a heaven now scratched with red.

"We're down this end," Walker said. "The room has a nice view of the meadow and the sea."

Pearl looked over his shoulder through a many-paned window at the ground below. To the west, just before the changing colors of the woods, was a swimming pool. To the north, a sandy cliff, a rocky beach and the sea. Various outbuildings were scattered behind meandering stone walls to the south, including a peculiar little stone house with a sod roof.

"Pearl," he said.

She followed him. His suit was a wonderful golden shade, like the meadow.

There was a brass bed in the room they entered. Some of the ornamentation on the headboard had been bent or broken. It was a spacious room. Walker's clothes hung in the closet. His hairbrush lay upon a pine bureau.

"I love you, Pearl," he said, smiling at her as though she were a foolish girl and this were all a joke.

"I . . . why . . . you think I'm just being silly here, don't you . . . just coming with you to your house." She tried to feel indignant, even frightened, but she could not. She was happy.

Walker ran his hand down across her breasts and rubbed her belly through her thin dress. She lay back on the white cotton bedspread, and he lay beside her, moving up her skirt, slipping off her pants. He dropped his big dark head upon her breasts. Pearl giggled. She lapped his ears like a puppy. She whispered her new love words. She loved it that they were dressed, that he covered her not with his nakedness but with the costume of propriety. She touched his belt, his hips, and then she closed her eyes and grasped the headboard, her fingers curling, one with the broken, cold design.

Later, she lay pressed against his back as he slept. The windows were open to the dark. Pearl could hear a child's voice rising from the bathroom below.

> "And may we, like the clock,
>   Keep a face clean and bright
>   With hands ever ready
>   To do what is right."

Pearl laughed. A clock chimed and Walker woke.

"Walker," a child cried from the other side of the door, "Thomas wants to meet Pearl."

"Ohh," Pearl murmured, "perhaps I should just stay up here for a few days until I get used to things. I'm a little slow at meeting people. I . . ."

"I'm awfully sorry," Walker said, "did I fail to introduce myself? I'm . . ."

"Ohh," Pearl said. She still felt happy. And full and energized after love.

Down in the library, Walker mixed her a drink from the bar. Pearl was happy with another person's happiness and daring. Walker handed her a glass and she swallowed her drink immediately. There were no children in the room; just two women and a man. Pearl suddenly felt nervous with another person's nervousness.

Walker made the introductions.

Shelly. My sister.

Miriam.

My brother, Thomas.

"What a beautiful skirt you're wearing," Pearl said to Miriam.

Miriam had a kind and leathery face and a graying braid that went down to her waist.

"Thank you," Miriam said.

Pearl was grateful. She sucked her drink.

"She makes them," Shelly said. "People send her scraps of material from everywhere."

"Tell us the story behind that common piece of blue there," Thomas said, pointing to a piece of serge fixed to Miriam's waistline.

"That," Miriam said instantly, "belonged to a young Australian seaman who was granted leave and flown home from Malta to assist his wife who was troubled by a black and white phantom without a head who kept punching her three children."

Pearl stared at the skirt. Its harmony was much too disassociative. And it was not beautiful although it was wonderfully done.

She looked away from the skirt to Thomas. He was a big dark man like Walker. He wore a rather grimy white linen suit and a white shirt. He had seemed like a dark, cold sun to Pearl.

"And what was that again, Miriam?" he asked, pointing to something quite ordinary, a white thing near the blue.

"That is from the pillowcase of a suicide."

"Goodness," Pearl protested.

"You must tell us something about yourself," Shelly said to

Pearl.

Pearl hadn't known anything to say about herself. She put her drink on the mantelpiece beside a little wooden sculpture there. There were several wooden carvings, all about four inches high. Nervously, she picked one up.

No one said anything. There was an enormous silence around her accentuated by the creak of a floor board.

"What *are* these things?" Pearl almost screamed, embarrassed. She extended her hand with the carving in it. It was an animal, a wolf. Pearl could see that. She had run her fingernail down its carved spine, where the carved hairs fell to either side. It was quite carefully done and it seemed charged with a sweaty energy in her damp hand. Its eyes and nostrils, the cloven sculpted sign of its sex, its teeth and haunches . . .

She dropped it on the rug.

Thomas picked it up and replaced it on the mantel.

"Aaron carved those, back in the 1800s," he said. "He made a dozen of them. Wolf, bear, fox, deer ... the animals he'd killed. In the beginning he was a hunter and a trapper. He knew a lot about animals. He ate them and collected them and skinned them and sold them. Then he began to re-create them."

"Did Aaron . . . was he the one who built this house?" Pearl put her empty hand around her drink.

"He and his wife, Emma. Aaron amassed considerable wealth in his time. That's why we're comfortable today. Were you wondering about that?"

"Oh no," Pearl said, "I wasn't ... no ..."

"He started off as a simple trapper but he was too smart for that occupation. The children will tell you though that he stopped killing because the last animal he dispatched spoke to him."

Pearl looked at Walker. She giggled. "What did it spoke?" she asked.

"It said, 'Why are you looking at me dying? Soon you will be an animal dying, and people will be looking at you.'"

Pearl said nothing. It seemed reasonable enough.

"Whatever it was, something changed his attitude. He cleaned himself up and got civilized. He made killings in the market place rather than the woods. Everything he touched was money. No one much liked him but he began to make too much money to be rejected. He bought into banks and railroads and steamboats ... he was part owner of the *Henry Clay*, the fastest steamboat on the Hudson until it burned and sank in 1852. It killed over a hundred people and Aaron was charged with manslaughter, but he was acquitted. Aaron was lucky. He was lucky until the day he died."

"Oh well," Pearl said vaguely.

"In his last years this is what he whittled with," Thomas said, lifting a short shallow box from behind the animals. He flicked it open with his thumbnail as though his nail were a key, exposing a short knife with a horn handle. The handle was carved with the images of sacrificed animals, a ring of endings, animal biting animal, twisting their way around the handle of the knife, body cavities being opened, throats being slit, vigorous animals, curiously peaceful, falling to their knees.

"Did he carve the handle too?" Pearl asked. "He was very good, wasn't he? I mean, he was a real artist, wasn't he?"

"No." Thomas smiled. "This is from the Yucatan, from the Mayan-Toltec period. Aaron was a collector. He liked nice things, extraordinary things."

"Was his wife extraordinary, his Emma?"

"Aaron married far beneath him," Thomas said.

Shelly smiled against her glass. Pearl moved closer to Walker.

"The children will tell you Emma was a witch," Thomas said.

Pearl stared at the fresh drink Walker had given her. "I don't believe in witches," she said.

"Why on earth would you?" Shelly asked.

"What about ghosts?" Thomas raised his brows indulgently.

He was looking at Pearl with the interest one usually reserves for dust.

"I thought this was supposed to be the adult hour," Shelly sighed.

"Many of my correspondents believe in ghosts," Miriam said.

"They live in foreign countries," Shelly said impatiently.

"Ghosts don't have access to this world, do they?" Pearl asked. "I mean they just remember it, don't they?"

Thomas laughed. "The children will get along fine with you, Pearl. They fancy the mysterious. They like to invent their own histories."

"I'd hate to think our history is as the children recollect it," Walker said. "The only odd relation I recall was the aunt who wanted to be a professional boxer."

"Oh God, yes," Thomas said.

"There are so many children here . . ." Pearl began.

"They come and go," Shelly said. "Thomas is always getting new ones."

"Well with so many of them and their birthdays . . . there must always be an occasion for a party . . ." The drinks had made Pearl feel gay.

"We celebrate everyone's birthday on a single day," Thomas said. "It makes things easier."

"For you maybe," Miriam protested. "I'm the one making the cakes. They can eat a cake apiece, I swear, and they all want different colored frostings and designs . . ."

"You love it, Miriam," Walker said.

"When are we going to eat?" Shelly said. "I'm off early tomorrow, you know, and I haven't packed a thing so far tonight."

"Fancy you asking about supper," Miriam grumbled, "you who never eat a thing."

"Shelly needs her energy," Thomas said. "She's off to college to get her mate."

"Oh honestly." Shelly blushed.

"Pick one that will make good babies," Thomas said.

They went into the dining room then. The children were summoned and everyone sat down. The children's faces were clean, their hair smacked down. They sat politely, serving one another. Thomas acted the role of catechist with them. There was much eager conversation which Pearl did not grasp very well. The drinks had made her dizzy and troubled. To see a child of six or seven running around like a wild animal one moment and sitting genteelly at the dinner table the next, discussing Meister Eckhart's formulations of transcendence into the nonself, was very disconcerting to Pearl.

She sighed. She raised a fork.

"Look, Pearl," a child said. His name was Johnny. His eyes looked old and tired and held an odd disintegration in their depths. He pushed a sea shell across the tablecloth to Pearl. "Hold it to your ear."

"Oh yes," she said, smiling. "I hear the ocean. I hear waves." The sea shell felt sticky and smelled sweet.

"No, you don't. You hear your own blood. That's the sound of your own blood singing in your ears." He took the shell back and put it on his lap. His face twitched nervously.

"Well," Pearl said, "I suppose."

A red-headed child with a rather large mouth sat beside Pearl. She ate quickly with swift, neat movements, and patted her mouth with her napkin after each mouthful.

"Emma got pregnant and had a baby that wasn't her own," she said to Pearl.

Children . . . their poor confusions, Pearl thought. "If she gave birth to the baby it had to be hers," Pearl said reasonably. "Sometimes men don't know if they're the father of the baby or not, but the mother has to know." She coughed. She felt she was getting in a little over her head.

The children across the table looked at her, interested. They shook their heads.

"No," a little boy named Trip said. He had a long thin face with a birthmark on his cheek. "No, Emma's baby wasn't hers."

Pearl smiled. "Emma's someone you've made up, isn't she?"

"No, no, Pearl," the red-headed girl said. "She's Walker's great-grandmother. And Thomas'. And Shelly's and Miriam's too."

"Well," Pearl said, "what happened to the baby that wasn't hers? She loved it just the same, didn't she?"

The children looked at her slyly.

"It got took back," they said together.

The gentle way they've appropriated death, Pearl thought.

"Oh that's very sad," she said. She looked down at her plate from which the design of a fish gaped at her and swam beneath her untouched food.

"When Emma died, nobody heard a token," an older girl said.

"Token? I don't . . . what's a token?"

"A token is the sound that tells you when somebody you know has gone. Sometimes it's a knock on the door and you open the door and nobody's there. And sometimes it's the sound of an owl coming from some place where there aren't any birds. It's a way people have of telling you they're dead."

Pearl looked at the little boy who had worn the feathers in his hair. His name was Peter.

"You should drink your milk," Pearl said.

"Magicians don't drink milk." He chewed on a piece of fish and, grimacing, took a sliver of bone from his mouth.

Pearl looked around the table into the intricacy, the darkness of the children's faces. She was relieved that she hadn't come to this place years before, when they had all been babies. Now that would have been too shocking, really. She suddenly saw them like that, screaming and laughing, blond-headed or bald, all being kept and cared for by the big, odd man at the head of the table. What a corrupt thought. Pearl made an odd, constricted gesture with her hands, pushing, in her mind, against the welter of children. Thomas looked up at her, holding a knife and fork in midair. He ate like a European, without switching hands. He watched her coolly, and embarrassed, she dropped her eyes.

When she and Walker were back in their room again, Pearl curled up on the bed. Her stomach ached. The white spread was dirty with footprints.

"Oh, my feet are disgusting," she said, kicking off her sandals. "Look at that. Awful. I'll be better, Walker, really I will."

He shrugged. He gave her some Bourbon in a glass. It sparkled warmly from within the glass. In her stomach, it burned.

They undressed and lay beneath the sheets. Walker made love to her. It felt good. Pearl's cries were channeled by the house's ducting. The children lay on the transoms in the dark, mute as rugs, listening.

"I don't think they like me here," Pearl said later, sleepily.

"The children adore you, Pearl."

"I mean . . . the grownups."

"Of course they do," he said. He caressed her face.

CHAPTER FOUR

Now, in Miami, Walker's caress pushed her halfway across the room. Pearl tried to view the situation objectively. Perhaps Walker had not actually struck her. Nevertheless, she found herself sprawled on her back in the corner. And yet ... she might have fallen on her own accord. She might have had a little too much to drink. The baby wasn't in her arms anymore.

Walker stood over her.

"How did you find me?" she asked.

"Darling, I'm forever tracking you. Now this is twice I've found you. I'm tiring of it." He spoke softly and helped her up. Her wrists hurt where he held them. "You must stop worrying about why things happen and wonder what they mean when they do."

"But how did you find me?" Pearl asked, bewildered.

"You've been muttering about leaving ever since Sam was born. You've been depressed. Thomas suspected you were depressed enough to do something like this."

"I went into town to buy Sam some little shirts," Pearl said vaguely.

"When you didn't come back over with Joe, we checked the air shuttles to Boston. And of course you had been on one. And then we simply checked with Boston. You talked about Miami, Pearl. You talked about leaving. It took no psychic to find you."

"But I thought I used the name 'Tuna.'"

"Tuna?"

"Listen, Walker," Pearl said, "I don't mind living with you but I don't want to live with your family."

"You're not yourself, Pearl."

"I am myself!" Pearl cried. "I am certainly myself." Big tears rolled down her cheeks. "I will kill myself, Walker," she said.

Walker sighed.

"I don't want to go back there," she said. "Tell me about Johnny. I want to know how Johnny is."

"He died this morning."

"See, see . . ." Pearl wept.

"That is something to cry about, Pearl, it's true."

"That child's blood is on Thomas' hands," she said. "It may be invisible to you but I see it there."

"Stop it," Walker said. He was tired and angry. He took off his sports jacket and draped it over a chair. He unbuttoned his cuffs and rolled up his sleeves. Pearl had a peculiar feeling, wondering if he were about to beat her up. She sat down on the bed, folding her hands carefully in her lap. She must be very drunk, she thought. Thomas had once told Pearl that when she drank too much she became stubborn, secretive and insulting. Thomas said that she behaved in a manner that elicited the possibility of ugly response.

Walker's voice was calm again. "You were very sick after you had Sam," he said.

"Your family makes me sick," Pearl said. "I don't want to live with them anymore. I want a normal life. I want a normal child."

"You can't raise this child by yourself," Walker said. "It's an absolute impossibility."

"I would get someone to help me," she said. "There are schools. I would send him to school. But before school I would get someone to help me and this person and I would play with Sam." Pearl's stomach hurt and her mouth was dry.

She wondered if she could get to the telephone and tell the

desk there was a man she did not know in her room. He was in her room and he was frightening her.

Pearl picked up the phone. Walker held her wrist with one hand until she put it back. With the other hand, he traced the bones of her jaw.

Pearl had once believed that she had the freedom to think about her circumstance in any way she chose, but she now realized that this was not the case. Freedom was an illusion even when one's instincts were good and Pearl lacked instincts of any kind. The few simple beliefs and inherited moralities that she had adopted from her parents were as inadequate guides for her own life as they had been for theirs. Her mother, who was a Baptist, told her that she should not eat cookies in the bathroom because God would not like it. She told her that she should keep the top of her bookcase dusted even though no one could see the top of her bookcase because God would see it and judge her. She told her that she could be interested in the Devil as long as she did not allow the Devil to become interested in her. Her mother had been sentimental and kind-hearted. She had taught Pearl how to braid her own hair and how to arrange wild flowers in a vase. Then one Sunday at a church coffee hour, bustling about the pantry, she had run herself through with a knife that had recently been sharpened for the exigencies of frozen food.

It seemed unrealistic. Pearl's father took it unrealistically. He took to drinking all night long in the dark. In the daytime, he walked around his property, putting his hands on the trunks of trees and saying, "I like these people."

Pearl trailed around after him, her eyes downcast.

"They're only vegetables, Daddy," she would say miserably.

Pearl had become very nervous in her father's presence because she could see quite clearly in his face that he was going to die soon. Near the end he talked about little except his grandmother, who had been a balloonist in Europe. He described her as a plain but intrepid little person with a neurotic fear of noise and of riding in carriages, who delighted in making night ascents for her own pleasure. He also said that as a child she had witnessed the murder of a Negro on the streets of Alabama.

At the very end he wanted to discuss Pearl's mother again. Of course they had both loved her. And where did Pearl think Mother was now? he had asked Pearl on that dreadful night. Pearl usually hemmed and hawed and tried to be noncommittal in her father's presence, being both shy and terrified of his dying look, but that night she confessed that, secretly, she saw her mother enfolded in wonderful wings, hovering over her every action. She saw her quite literally with an aura fragrant and golden and big as the house.

And what did Pearl think about death? her father asked. What was her opinion there? And encouraged by his calmness and his interest, Pearl said that death in her mind was mixed up with an image of a person opening a bulkhead door and descending into the cellar as though for an armload of kindling or a jar of tomato jam. The image was an amiable one. Her mother and father had always told her that she was an amiable sweet child, but when Pearl said this, her father had looked at her with real disgust.

"Life," he had said, "is tears, blood, sin, sperm and excrement. And death," he had screamed, "is the same thing!"

Pearl's feelings had been quite hurt. Her father had never screamed at her before and she felt that it was quite an inappropriate time to be screaming such things about death when one was so ill and sick in spirit. There then fell a grim silence between them. Her father finally broke it by making himself another drink. He then walked to the garage, where he picked up his shotgun. Sipping his drink, he then walked around to the back of the house where he kicked the spring snow off the catches and opened the bulkhead door.

"Daddy," Pearl called timidly.

But her father didn't speak to her again. He went into the cellar and shot himself in the mouth.

Pearl's life had never lacked in gesture but it had always avoided significance. It avoided meaning as the bird does the snare. Nothing in her life had prepared Pearl for significance. Each moment that occurred lay mute within her, a buried stone, contained from and irrelevant to herself, an event with neither premonition nor consequence. She couldn't imagine incorporating what was determined as yesterday into what was considered tomorrow. She saw herself as a little child still, the bourn of all her mother's hopes. Sitting in this room, not nearly as drunk as she would like to be with a man who seemed more surgeon than husband, the surgeon with whom one would go into one's last, unsuccessful operation.

"You shouldn't drink so much, Pearl," the surgeon said. "You think you're being revived when you're only being deluded."

Pearl slid off the bed and looked into the crib, where Walker had put the baby. Sam was there in a snug, blue sleeper. He seemed to be chuckling. He was beautiful. He had a nice complexion, like Walker's. She wanted to feel calm, looking after her baby, but all she could feel were the arguments between her and Walker, going back and forth. The air in the room seemed moiling with the arguments. She imagined small dark creatures crouched in the corners of her head, making insults and promises.

She looked at Walker. "If you could just give me a little time away from the ... your family."

"Why do women always talk about wanting a little time?" Walker asked. "It really annoys the shit out of me."

"You're exactly like Thomas," Pearl said faintly. "You're cruel and overbearing ... and unrealistic."

"Unrealistic," Walker said, astonished. "Unrealistic."

"It means, I mean ... to think that I would go back with you just because you happened to find me."

"I could certainly let you go," Walker said. "You could stay here in Florida and get skin cancer, catch lobsters with your bare hands, fuck yard boys. I could take Sam back and leave you here, but it would upset the children. They're amused by you, Pearl. They want you back."

She thought of the long year she had just spent there. The winter had been the worst. So much cold and so little daylight. They slept and slept like hibernating things. The children moved like shadows of their summer selves.

"Please," Pearl said wearily.

"You have no other plans," Walker said.

"I just got here. Things will fall together."

"No plans," he said. "Just mommy and new baby in a bright warm new world."

She said nothing.

"A mommy living by sensation rather than intention."

"That's right," Pearl said.

"You're a woman who's just birthed a son and you feel close to the great convulsive power, the life force."

She blushed. It was true. When she wasn't frightened or in despair, she felt quite smug. The Amazons took crescent-shaped shields into battle with them. The symbols of womanhood offer less protection than most.

"You think, when you don't think about it much, that you understand everything."

"Everything is pretty understandable if you take away what people do to you and the shapes they assume and what they say," Pearl said bleakly.

Walker came close to her, put his arms around her, caressed her buttocks. "Your world is one of bodily urges and meanings. You don't understand anything," he said.

"I'm not coming back there with you," Pearl said.

"You're not going anyplace else," he said lightly.

"Oh don't threaten me," she said, annoyed. "That doesn't matter to me, you know. I don't care about that anymore."

But there was a rumble of panic underneath everything. And if it wasn't the fear of death, what was it? She felt it always, the terror, even in the brightest moments. What was it then, when she didn't even care?

Pearl pulled away from him.

She felt a pain of incompleteness and indecision. Her breasts hurt from nursing. With the hurt she woke into a terrible fright. She remembered a little stove her mother had made for her when she was a child. A packing crate with circles painted on top of it to indicate gas rings. She had played with it dutifully. Accepting the game and love's deceit. When her father had taken her fishing, he had equipped her with a rod and line that had a big screw eye on the end instead of a hook. They had been protecting her. They had been afraid of accident. They had provided her with substitutions and she had lived safely in the brightness of false things.

She feared that her mother and father had died, that they weren't with her anymore. She said their names aloud.

"It's true," Walker said soothingly. "It was years ago."

It was a terrible fear. It was terrible for her to worry so about the dead. Her heart pounded. There were car wrecks and diseases. The dead were in danger of dying. The fear was like a storm within her, a storm unalive and yet with a dreadful will for destruction . . .

"You're all alone," Walker said. "You have no one but us."

"It doesn't matter," Pearl said. "It doesn't matter that I'm alone. And I'm not alone."

"Your mind is an amazing thing to hear working," Walker said.

"I have Sam."

"We have Sam," Walker said. "Sam's going to be wonderful."

"I don't like you," Pearl said, defeated.

Walker grunted. "You used to like it," he said.

"'It' was you once."

"You should get out a little more, Pearl. You've become too self-obsessed. Get off the island a bit. Don't go far. Go to Morgansport and have your hair done. Go to a movie. Go to the fairgrounds and ride the wooden horses."

Pearl remembered the wooden horses. The merry-go-round was the oldest in America. The horses had real teeth, and tails made of real hair. The children had taken her to see them once. The children had also taken her to see a movie at the firehouse which she would have sworn was pornographic. The children had taken her to a museum which consisted of Rimbaud's suitcase and an Ethiopian assassin's trigger finger in a glass jar.

Pearl had been to Morgansport three times. She couldn't imagine what she had been doing with her days. She had stayed on the island but what had she done? She had talked with the children or thought about the children or walked with the children outside between the stone walls that meandered everywhere. Walls which ended often in enclosures from which anything could escape. The walls everywhere, in the cleared land and the tangle, keeping things neither in nor out. The stones forever giving way and being rearranged in the children's play.

Walker was talking on the telephone. He was making arrangements. A cab was going to pick them up and take them to the airport.

"I don't want to have any more children, Walker."

"All right."

"A woman has only one child," Pearl said. "All the rest are false ones."

"Poor Pearl," Walker said. "We'll be home around two A.M."

Pearl wanted another drink. The room shuddered. It contracted and expanded. She watched the baby in the crib, churning his arms in the air, striking the crib slats with his sacked feet.

"I like Sam," Pearl said, waving her hand at him. "I don't want him to grow up and be peculiar."

"It's your behavior that seems peculiar, Pearl. It's you who walk the streets looking both unhappy and unconvinced. The people of Miami will arrest you if you appear unhappy and unconvinced here. They do not respect sickness in Miami. This isn't your sort of place."

Walker's voice was often pleasant even when he was saying hurtful things. She wanted to put her arms around him, to topple with her arms around him off that moment's brink and into nothingness.

She looked at the baby. He gazed back, small chest heaving, his face stern. She unbuttoned her blouse and picked him up and put him to her breast. He made loud smacking noises. The nipple stood out long and wet. She kissed the top of his head. When he finished, she gave him to Walker. They went down into the lobby to wait for the cab.

CHAPTER FIVE

The plane they were to take back north was about half full. There were several weary families with small children aboard. Pearl felt that she looked like any of the young mothers there, drawn, quiet, wanting to get on with it. The seats were three abreast. Pearl sat down wearily at the window. Walker buckled himself into the aisle seat. The baby lay on a pillow between them.

"I'd like a martini, please," she said.

"They don't serve drinks until we're in the air."

"I am not an imaginative person, Walker, nor am I a suggestible person. But in a dream, if something was unpleasant, I would cover my eyes with my hands and I would just withdraw from that dream. I wouldn't wake up but I would just go into another dream. I became so good at that, Walker. It was my one talent really. I wish I could do that in real life."

"Oh for Christ's sakes," Walker said, "'real life.'"

"I know I don't express myself well, Walker, but I'm depressed."

"Yes, certainly," Walker said.

Pearl took a deep breath. She said, "The body is a corpse, Walker, just a corpse and it is only the soul that keeps it from putrefaction and I feel that my soul is gone now. That it has been gone for about a year now actually. I feel that all those children have it in some way."

"The children have their own souls, Pearl."

"I feel . . ."

"You just have the postpartum blues, Pearl. It's nice to have children. Children make us eternal."

"That's a Jewish conceit, isn't it? Because they don't believe in resurrection. No, no, that's not what I'm saying at all, Walker." She looked at him mournfully. "I have to go to the bathroom," she said.

Walker got up and stood in the aisle to let her pass.

"Why don't you sit over there," she said, gesturing toward the window. "I don't feel well, I might have to get up now and then."

Pearl made her way to the back of the plane. The aisle was congested with people stowing their possessions away. At the back of the plane was another baby, this one in the arms of a very old woman. Pearl stood beside them as she waited to get into the toilet. The old woman was opening her mouth and closing it at the baby. The baby was listening intently. They were obviously two individuals who understood each other. The woman was the oldest person Pearl had ever seen in her life. You would think that they'd refuse to transport a person in that condition through the air. Well, life is a mystery, Pearl thought. She looked at the old woman's strong, bony skull visible through the thin hair. It certainly was odd that such an ancient woman would be in charge of such a tiny baby. Pearl stared at them. The baby slowly unfixed its eyes from the old woman and stared at Pearl. They were golden, gelid eyes. Pearl felt bewitched. She couldn't help herself. Being a mommy made of her a loose species. She crooked her index finger and passed it softly, affectionately, over the baby's mouth.

The old woman slowly pulled the baby out of reach and wiped his face on the sleeve of her sweater.

"I'm sorry," Pearl said. Old people were particular about things. They worried about diseases. "I have a baby too. I . . ." She turned and walked back to her seat, not remembering why she had left it.

"Feeling better?" Walker asked.

Pearl said, "Do you believe that you can tell a transformed person by its eyes?"

"Pardon me?" Walker said.

"Haven't you heard the children with their werewolf talk? Peter and Trip? They've spoken of nothing else for weeks. They found a book or something. Haven't you heard them? Is it just me they talk to? All that stuff about people vomiting fingers and dogs' paws. All that stuff about the souls of animals infusing themselves into the trunks of men . . ."

Walker rubbed his forehead with his hand

"Did you know for instance that, long ago, people executed animals for crimes they believed they committed in the guise of men? That they conducted proper trials and formally hung beasts? And if the creature was unfortunate enough to be caught in his crime while he was still affecting the appearance of the man, his body was often torn apart by those convinced that they would find the body of a beast inside . . ."

"Pearl," Walker said.

"And those plays they put on! Children shouldn't be doing that. Children should be throwing Frisbees or something. Those plays! They say it's mostly Shakespeare. *Mostly*. I don't believe it. They're always killing one another.

> 'What means this bloody knife?
> 'Tis hot, it smokes
> It came even from the heart of . . .'"

"Pearl," Walker said. "Be quiet for a moment."

The door to the flight deck had closed on the crew and the plane was taxiing into the position for take-off. From the window, she could see several other big planes strung in a semicircle behind them.

Pearl held Walker's arm. She moved his fingers to her lips. His hands were hot, velvety, as though the blood were burning fiercely there.

"It's just that I want you to see my point. Those children could drive a person crazy. They make their little worlds . . . it's a terrible thing to see . . ." Her voice was rising. A teen-ager with a flimsy mustache and army camouflage trousers looked at her in gentle alarm. The trousers would have merged perfectly with a sofa her mother had once, Pearl thought.

Pearl sighed. She rested her head against the starched white napkin pinned to the top of her seat.

Every four weeks the moon is swallowed by a hostile pig. So the children would say, giggling. And so what, so what! As good a way as any for explaining why it wasn't out that night.

Pearl stroked the baby Sam's hair absent-mindedly. He was sleeping. None of the roaring that filled her ears bothered him in the slightest. It was night. Nights were all right. Now the mornings she was more suspicious of. The way the light *sneaked* up on you. And that *gap* between dawn and sunrise! Who could make preparations for a sneaky light like that? Who could make amends?

Her father had once told her, on a day when they were all alive, that she had magic mittens magnetic to snow.

The flaps of the plane's wings were raised. The extensive minute machinery was visible. An arrogant complexity. Unseemly. Railing against heaven.

They were all imprisoned here, in this plane's fragile shell. Pearl realized with abrupt clarity that the plane was going to crash. They had left the ground now. The sound of the engines was high and steady. They were climbing. But Pearl knew that they would crash. They were too low, somehow flying beneath the horizon. She held Walker's hand.

In school she had learned that the edge of the universe had been sighted. Dutifully, she had copied in her notebook the manner in which this was told. *The edge of the universe would represent the first accumulations of matter in an evolving cosmos. The matter is seen by looking a great distance through space and hence into the past.*

The notebook had long ago been lost. She was no student. And yet now this page, these words, blazed in her mind's eye—a signpost to a chaos so complete, so ordered, that she glimpsed the lunatic face of God.

She dropped Walker's hand and picked up the baby.

She hugged her knees and pressed her forehead against the back of the seat in front of her. Off the coast of Madagascar, inhabiting the depths of the sea, live obsolete fish which have never kept their appointment with extinction. Something, again, her father had told her in the days when they were all alive.

Three minutes after take-off from Miami, the pilot flew serenely into the aurora of grasses that was the Everglades. The plane skated briskly for a moment and then nosed heavily into the mud. The right wing was sheared off and partially entered the cabin, almost separating the plane in two, opening it up like a child's hinged and portable toy. Pearl felt herself torn from the seat and flying awkwardly, belly-up, through the air. Perhaps this really was the way the dying did it. Imagine. Being depicted accurately all these years by the visionaries. One simply spread one's arms and flew home.

She saw Walker, forced backward, his thick hair opening up, letting in the night. Her arm fluttered toward him but her fingers could not hold to his shoulder. She had lost all contact with the baby.

She fell from the air with a painful crack and lay on her back, a hundred feet from the plane, water running into her eyes, a heavy weight on her chest. The light in the swamp was faintly lavender. Everything was smoking. The grass stank terribly. She plucked at the weight on her chest weakly. It seemed like something she could push away. But it was nothing. The bodice of her dress stuck to her fingers and came away in shreds. Something crawled away from her on all fours, screaming. She kept plucking at her chest, fretting about the weight now, wanting it, wanting it to become the baby's weight. The sky possessed the faintest, most delirious color, casting a glow upon the scene that it brought it out of darkness certainly but not into any sort of light. Sections of the fuselage burst into flame and extinguished themselves in almost the same moment. Flesh and metal had fused, and damaged and distorted objects gave no clue as to what they once had been but everything seemed cruelly, senselessly alive. A man stood not far from Pearl, standing very straight, seemingly uninjured, and screaming, screaming, although she heard no sound.

Pearl struggled to turn on her side, on her stomach, to search with the rest of the living for that which was lost. Two dogs, pets that were being transported in the luggage bay, loped past her, whining. One returned, circled her, sniffed her head and then ran on. Pearl clutched at the grass that supported her but her arms sank into the muck almost up to her elbows. She crouched, swaying, and, finally with great effort, got to her feet. She felt like a savage, drooling slightly, incapable of decision.

She heard her own voice absurdly calling the baby's name. And then Walker's name. Her mouth was swollen. The words were meaningless even to her own ears. She had brought this disaster down upon them with her foolishness, her selfishness. She stumbled on through the swamp. A shoe was missing and part of the skin on her right arm. The plane was bright and barren in the moonless night. People were moving now. There was yellow smoke everywhere. The sky was yellow. There were lights in the sky dropping straight down.

She brushed against something and shrank back. The thing wafted against her bare arm. It was crisp, yet feathery, the seared wing of some large wading bird. Killed in its own domain by the impact of the crash, it lay across Pearl's path, charred yet whole, its long elegant legs crisscrossing Pearl's own, its brutal beak discreetly shut. A fishing feeding creature whose destiny had crossed a more powerful and inept one. Pearl gagged. Her legs seemed caught in the thing's legs.

She saw a wig floating in the mud. Several wigs.

She crawled away from the bird. "Walker!" she screamed. Walker. Walker. She had lain with him and made a baby. She had punished them all.

Suddenly, her ears seemed to open up to holocaust. Airboats with huge spotlights were floating across the grass toward the wreckage. And the sounds of the injured were inhuman. But familiar, like the cries of the owls at home. WAUGH-O WAUGH-O. Owls feeding on the abundant meat of despair.

Healthy men were moving around her now. Men who were intact. She passed the young camouflaged boy still strapped into his seat. One eyebrow was half torn off and fluttered from his face. There was a sloppy dark stain around his waist where the seatbelt cinched him in.

Pearl saw the dogs again, running ahead of her, bumping into things as though they were blind.

"My baby," Pearl said. "Please, I had a baby. Please give me back my baby. He was in my arms."

A man brushed by her almost knocking her down. She grabbed his arm. "There's a baby here," she said. "You must find it. It's my baby."

He looked at her hopelessly. "All right," he said. "Stay right here, don't move from here."

He left. But she was nowhere. She was beside nothing. No landmark. The owls, or something in the swamp, kept moaning. An owl's nest was full of everything. All food for their grief. Trout, rabbits, thrushes. Balls of hair and bones with rings attached. WAUGH-O WAUGH-O. She was calling Walker's name again and then the child's. "Please," she called, "I have a baby. He's here."

Pearl sat down. The swamp sucked at her sides. She folded her arms across her lap as though she were holding something there. Then she felt it in her arms, something trembling, small, and other arms around her, carrying her, hurriedly but not without care. She was on a stretcher now, with a blanket lying loosely across her, and pressed against her troubled heart was a living infant boy.

CHAPTER SIX

In the hospital nursery the baby lay, covered with ointment and lying on greased paper, prepared much like fish *en papillote*. He twitched occasionally in sleep, rosily singed, every bit of hair burned off his head from the crash.

On the floor above, in a private room, lay Pearl, her ribs and arm bandaged and a square of gauze taped to her forehead. She lay with her eyes squeezed, against the pillow.

Walker was dead.

She lay with her eyes squeezed shut trying to resurrect him. Memory is the resurrection. The dead move among us the living in our memory and that is the resurrection.

Pearl had never had much faith. Her mother's favorite hymn kept intruding upon her compilation of Walker's images.

> Ohhhhhh He walks with me
> And He talks with me
> And He tells me I am His owwwwwwn

Christianity was too carnal for Pearl. She turned and lay on her back.

Once Walker had taken her on a jeep ride across the island. There were three or four children bouncing along with them. Blueberries fell from the bushes and into the jeep like rain. The ecstatic children hung panting over the sides, almost falling, their lips rolled back over their gums, their eyelids fluttering with smashed webs.

Steaks lowed beneath the trees. The bones of fishes banged in their sockets like guns going off. There were the sounds of doors slamming that were like the sounds of traps being sprung.

She flapped open her eyes to a smooth white ceiling.

She would never again remember Walker as she had seen him. He had flown out of the wilderness dreary into the night. Into Paradise, her mother would have said.

God loves you, her mother had said. God loves us all. And He takes us in the end with him to Paradise where we find refuge forever from sin and affliction and doubt.

Pearl suspected God didn't love human beings much. She suspected that what He loved most was Nothingness.

God created everything out of nothing and He takes us back again to feed the nothingness that He loves.

It was pretty sick of Him, Pearl thought. God wasn't dead, He was just sick. Very very sick . . .

This was grief, she guessed. All these terrible things and thoughts rooting around in her head, trying to find a place to stay.

She saw another man in the brass bed she had shared with Walker . . . the bed with the ornate headboard to which she had raised her arms, her legs in love. A man with a penis half iron and half flesh . . . And forked beautifully like a serpent's tongue so that he would be able to perform all the acts of love at once . . .

"No!" Pearl said. A bird with black wings nested in her left eye. With her right eye she saw the hospital room where she knew she was awake.

She saw Walker looking like Thomas, pulling her down to take her breath away. A dead person who loves you will love you forever and ever . . .

A nurse in the room was plumping up Pearl's pillow.

"Would you like to see your baby now?" she said cheerily. "Are you up to nursing him? He just woke up and he's howling like a polecat. He won't take to a bottle at all."

"No," Pearl said. "He's never had a bottle."

Lucky little baby, little Sam. Other children had died in the same crash. Amazing grace. The ways of fate. It's a blessing we can't comprehend them.

Pearl unbuttoned her hospital shirt.

"Your brother-in-law just arrived," the nurse said. "You'll probably be released tomorrow."

Pearl bit her lip.

"Can't I stay here a little longer?" Pearl said.

"Modern medicine can't do a thing for cracked ribs, honey. And your baby, little Sandy . . ."

"Sam!" Pearl said, worried. "His name is Sam."

"Oh, I'm sorry, honey, we got so many of them down there, you know, and they each got a name and I've got just one poor brain."

"Sam," Pearl said.

"Well, little Sam looks as though he's just got a bad sunburn is all. Nothing worse than that. You don't want to be taking beds from those that really need them now, do you, honey?" The nurse cranked up the bed and left.

Pearl sat tensely staring at the door. When Thomas saw her, what would he say to her? You're loathsome. That's what he'd say. She was loathsome. She was an idle, stupid woman, no more incremental to his world than a gnat. She wouldn't blame him at all. She wished she were dead, leading her own life at last, singing the old hymns.

> And the joy we share as we tarry there
> No other has ever knoooooown

She could see Thomas, talking with the doctors, paying the bill, signing the papers. She could see his eyes behind his dark glasses, black with anger, with rage at her.

It had now been hardly more than thirty-six hours since she had left the island. And now with all this, with Walker dead, she was going back. And Sam would be raised there, along with the rest. Pearl saw Peter causing a baby chick to rise from his scrambled eggs. She saw Joe kissing a girl with a tongue heavy as a boot. She saw the children running and waiting.

In the house was an eighteenth-century Goddard-Townsend desk. Someone wanted to buy the desk for a hundred thousand dollars. Someone wanted Thomas to run for governor. But there were scratches and gouges in the desk, made by the children. And Thomas, when angry, could not hold his temper very well. A woman, someone familiar, was smiling at him and saying, "Ahhh, if spit were sperm ..."

Shelly was saying, "I don't know how my own brother, Walker, who was so smart, could have married a woman with a brain so small it would get lost in a cat's fur ..."

Miriam was sewing her terrible dark skirts, the skirts that depicted all the fears of the night. "I don't believe in love anymore," she was saying, "not since Johnny died." Miriam loved Johnny and what good had that ever done? Her feeling for her Johnny was curved as a ball, a belly, a noose. There was no beginning to it. No end. Come unbidden. Part pain. Part comfort. That was love. How could that be the way? To love was only to understand death. And Pearl was saying, looking at the skirts, seeing the story of the skier who had caused an avalanche that buried fourteen, and the society painter who painted vulvas, and the woman whose twin had lain inside her for twenty-nine years and would not be born, and other stories, other images which could not be grasped by reason or even madness, collected in those skirts that hung like the robes of priests in the closets of the house Pearl was seeing, and saying that the path illuminated by death is the true path, that it is the knowledge of death which shapes us, which gives us the form by which we shall be known. Which divides us from the animals.

The nurse was holding Sam out to Pearl. He was a ball of fierce red howling in a receiving blanket.

Pearl looked at him uncertainly. For two months now she had been feeding him, making faces at him, always checking to see if he was wet. Children had never seemed reasonable to Pearl. They grew up. They vanished without having died.

She took Sam and put him to her breast.

"What a yum-yum," the nurse said. "I'll leave you two alone now."

"You hungry, Sam?" Pearl whispered. "Poor little baby. You're safe now."

She fanned her nipple against his cheek. He reached for her breast with his small hands and began kneading it. His eyes were shut tight. He began fiercely to draw upon the milk.

"Ow," Pearl winced.

She wriggled up higher against the pillows, trying to make herself more comfortable. The baby clung to her, chewing.

"Oh you're starved, aren't you?" Pearl said. She pushed him up, trying to relieve the pain. "Maybe I've forgotten how to do this, stupid Pearl can't do any ..." She cried out again. There was a spot of blood on her nightshirt, another on the baby's chin. She held her breath. The baby was making enraged snuffling sounds, his face flat and distorted against her breast. It was very embarrassing. She wanted to tear the baby from her breast. Her breast was bleeding. She slipped her fingers between her nipple and his gums and tried to push him off.

"You're ready for hamburger, aren't you?" Pearl said. She wanted to be calm. She wanted to show her good sense and wit.

A sharp pain ran jagged from her breast to her groin. She screamed and wrenched the baby's head from her. She slid off the bed and stared at Sam. He had kicked off the blanket and lay kicking and whimpering, his black, blurred eyes encompassing the room.

Pearl quickly pushed up the sides of the bed so he wouldn't roll out. He was quite helpless really. She backed up to the visitor's chair by the window and sat down. She looked at her breast. It was bruised and dotted with pinpoints of blood. She dabbed at it with a tissue.

Sam struggled and kicked inside his little sleeping sack. He clutched the edge of the pillow slip in his fist. Pearl stared at him. On the window sill were the remains of her lunch. She picked up a roll and, going back to the bed, opened his fist and closed it around the bread. He pushed it against his mouth and began to eat. When he had eaten about half of it, he fell asleep.

It seemed quite clear to Pearl that her child had something wrong with him. His face was all right, the little bit of him that showed, that wasn't encapsulated in soft cotton, in the cuddly devices of infant clothes. To the eyes of a stranger, in fact, he might seem a very handsome baby. Strangers recognized only what they were used to recognizing in a baby's face anyway.

She unzipped his long shirt.

"I don't think you're the right kind of baby," Pearl said softly. His skin was loose and rather wrinkled and covered with fine, almost invisible hairs.

She looked at his small hands, the tiny sharp nails, his smooth face, now calm. His face was like a mask's, like a small animal's.

Perhaps she had never looked at him this carefully before. She felt lightheaded. On the baby's hand were two small circular birthmarks. Sam had had a birthmark but it hadn't been there, had it? Hadn't it been on his chest?

"I'm having a breakdown is all," Pearl whispered.

She knelt on the floor and threw up in a bedpan. Then she sat back down in the chair by the window. Outside, the air quivered with the warmth of the sun. What would she do when the night came? How would she bear the night?

"You're not my baby," she said. "You belong to someone else." She pressed her fingers against her lips. "No, no, no," she said. She wanted to hold the baby and rock him in her arms but she was afraid to. There seemed to be a great pressure on her head from the four corners of the room.

"I'm having a breakdown is all," she muttered again.

An old woman stood on the room's threshold. Her chin rested, quivering, on her chest. Her skinny arms in the loose bathrobe were outstretched. She made a strange, whining noise.

She moved off when the nurse appeared.

"Nobody ever stays in their bed around here," the nurse said. "I think we should strap you all down." It was a different nurse, one with a round, mannish face, and a very pink, gorgeously repugnant nose.

"Who was that?" Pearl demanded. "She was about to come in here!"

"Probably wanted to steal something from you," the nurse said blithely. "They'd rather thieve than watch television. Television's gotten too dirty for them."

It was just an old woman, Pearl thought. Florida was full of them. Florida had more old women than it did grapefruit.

The nurse was looking at Sam.

"I couldn't feed him," Pearl said. "He has to be weaned, I have no milk."

"All right, all right," the nurse said. "I don't know why you'd choose to have him hanging off you anyway. I find it almost offensive, to be frank. Down here you see them suckling in laundromats, at the movies, everywhere."

She picked up the baby and started out. Sam yawned. Perfectly placed on either side in the upper gums were tiny triangular teeth.

The nurse sighed. "God help us," she said. "He's starting early. The things I've seen coming in and going out of this place. It makes me believe what I read. Have you read those things, about mankind's physiognomy? We're going to be taller and balder with bigger heads and smaller eyes and no jaws to speak of. It's pollution, they say. It's the Cubans as far as I'm concerned. God, I'm getting sick of the Cubans. I just bless God I'm not going to be around in fifty years. I wouldn't want to be in your shoes for anything, having a child in this day and age."

She left with the baby. Pearl sat stunned, once more alone. After a while she got up and picked up the bedpan. She went out into the hall to the bathroom to rinse it out. There were people a lot worse off than she was, certainly, lying about in every room. She went into the bathroom. She wanted to take a shower, to soak away the pain she felt, but she'd been told not to get her rib bandages wet. She looked longingly at the cold white of the curtainless stalls. She suddenly had the peculiar sensation that there was someone behind her wanting to get by, but she turned and there was no one. It was like a movement that had no counterpart in life flowing into the empty space around her. A vivid energy struggling to become a form. A starving shadow. Pearl pressed her forehead against the white tiles. She felt as though she were spinning.

She pushed herself away from the wall and started back down the corridor. She couldn't seem to find her room. The one she thought was hers was occupied by another old woman in a brown, mottled bathrobe. Pearl walked to the end of the corridor, bewildered. She decided to go down to the nursery on the floor below and look at the babies. It seemed a brilliant idea to her. Things would have a chance to straighten themselves out. She went down a short flight of thick green steps. On the landing was a Dr. Pepper bottle and a paperback novel with a lurid cover. The man on the cover did not look at all like Walker. Pearl remembered being kissed but it seemed a very long time ago. Walker's mouth was warm and smooth. It was the gold in his teeth.

She went down a few more steps and pushed open the door.

There was a sweet, vaguely punishing smell. The walls were bright landscapes populated by cheerful animals engaged in human endeavors. Part of the wall, beneath the nurses' station, was sketched in but not painted yet. It was filled with ghostly rabbits. Oh, to be a child, Pearl thought, one with the magic and unutterable images. Childhood is a wonderful moment, a wonderful moment. One sees things differently there. She walked down the floor, a smile fixed upon her face. There, beyond the nursery window, were the babies. A nurse was rinsing the mattress of an empty crib with a wet cloth. The babies were sleeping, ten or so of them, hunkered bottoms-up in identical white smocks. Some of them were as bald as Sam and some of them were as red as he was. Pearl looked at them for a while and then turned away. She walked back toward the staircase door, passing several more rabbits, a burro, and the White Queen. The White Queen had howled before she'd been pinched, wasn't that it? Her memory worked forward as well as backward. Pearl stopped at a water cooler and drew a paper cone from the dispenser. Turning the spigot created a turbulence within the glass. The water surged and slapped against the sides and Pearl saw her fragmented, wavering face. She felt wretched, scarcely human herself. Perhaps the human race had yet to be born. Perhaps it was all a deception by the government. It hadn't happened yet. This life was nothing but the womb.

Pearl limped through the door again and up the stairs. Someone had taken the paperback. The room Pearl believed to be hers was empty now. She entered it with relief, closed the door behind her and lay down upon the bed. A clock on the wall said three o'clock. It seemed to Pearl that clocks always said three o'clock. Once someone had shown her a photograph of a child lying in a coffin. Pearl closed her eyes. Serious drinkers were drinking at a drinkers' party. There were toasts. Here's to them that shoot and miss, someone said. Everyone drank to that. We have dishonored the unknown, someone said. We have annihilated the spirit. Everyone drank.

Pearl looked at the clock again. It still said three o'clock. The time Christ died on the cross. Time for something to come around again. We have taken matters too much in our own hands. Pearl crossed her arms tightly across her breasts. When would they bring the baby back up to her? When would they tell her she had to leave with him? She and Thomas and the baby would go out into the heat, an unholy trinity of souls.

She had wanted Sam to be a simple child, her child. Not like the others with their peculiar scraps of knowledge, their dazzling shows of temperament. The others even with their many charms seemed like deadly little flowers to Pearl, budding Satans, quoting Dante before they lost their baby teeth, their days one interlocking game with rules Pearl couldn't begin to comprehend.

Pearl's eyes moved from the clock to the old woman looking into the room again. She was tall and gaunt and dressed in brown and faded clothes that seemed for all their drabness nevertheless miraculous. The old woman raised her arm and it was as though a bird had raised its wing and Pearl saw the pinions of the wing, the way each feather miraculously blended into another, the way each midnight heartless line in tapering thrust was more excellent, a thousand times more excellent than the most sincere aspirations of her soul.

It was the old woman from the plane, looking for her child, wanting him back.

"He's not here now," Pearl said.

Pearl was tired of living in this world. Things turned out badly in this world. Even if one had no desires and made few decisions, one's shadow fell in the paths of others and their shadows fell all over you.

Pearl groped for a hairbrush on the nightstand. She began brushing her hair. Her hair was matted and she brushed out several gray hairs she hadn't noticed the day before. They were wrinkly as wires. Pearl's eyes started crying. She had a baby. She had to stop being so self-conscious.

But there was something peculiar about the baby. He was like an animal. She had a baby now that wasn't hers.

The old woman had entered the room. Her eyes bored into Pearl's mind and Pearl kept seeing the eyes and the old woman beyond them in her mind. Pearl stopped brushing her hair and tried to fix the old woman's position in the room so that she could call the nurse and have her removed. But her position could not be fixed. The old woman was moving, searching around the room, flying around in Pearl's mind.

Pearl dropped the brush and gripped her breasts and her eyes and her head in one complex and despairing gesture.

Maybe it wasn't an old woman at all, neither from the plane nor anywhere else. Maybe it was just death. Death coming around to tell Pearl she'd messed up again.

CHAPTER SEVEN

After the crash, Pearl went into what could only be considered a decline. The young girl had become a dissipated woman, calm and acquiescent enough, but possessed of a grim, perplexed attitude and somewhat confusing in her speech. She spent most of her time either in her room or in a lawn chair by the pool, lacking the energy or interest to do anything else.

This was where the children gathered. The adults did not use the pool. Lincoln used the sauna for relaxation. Shelly did not swim. Miriam and Thomas were strong, old-fashioned swimmers who preferred the ocean.

Swimming was probably good for one's system or one's tone or whatever, but in any case it was a maniacally healthful habit that Pearl didn't indulge in, preferring personally to be a bit under the weather. For she had long been ignoring her appearance and cultivating her ill health, her flesh seeming quite useless to her now, being touched by no hands other than her own for so long now.

She had begun actually to take an intoxication in the wonder of her sickly body, the bony chest, the tanned but sickly face.

The pool was a considerable distance from the house, cupped naturally in the meadow as though it had been there forever. And indeed, it seemed unclear when exactly the pool had been constructed. Little Jesse, who as far as Pearl knew, spent his every waking moment paddling around in the water, would tirelessly ask the same question of everyone, year in and year out:

"Were you here when they dug the hole?"

"No," Pearl said.

It seemed simple enough. But no one else ever gave the child a straight answer. Sometimes they'd tell him they were and sometimes they'd tell him they weren't. Sometimes they'd tell him that trucks and tractors bigger that the biggest toy, all shiny and red and stinking of rubber came in, and sometimes they'd tell him that Miriam dug it out with a slotted spoon. And sometimes they'd tell him that the Devil made it, just as the Devil made them all, the Devil liking to make things even more than God.

The children would tease Jesse about being born in the water.

"Your mama peed in the pool and out came you," they'd sing.

Jesse didn't seem to mind their teasing. Perhaps he didn't even hear it. Perhaps he heard, as fish do, by echo, and the voices of the children were no more to him than familiar reverberations in a friendly sea.

"Your mama loved the water more than she did a man. Your mama ..."

No one knew who Jesse's mother was actually. Thomas had brought him from a Boston adoption agency. Thomas had been touched by his ugliness. Jesse was a curious little child with a huge barrel chest and skin that seemed puckerish and a watery blue. Even when he was dressed properly and eating with them in the formal dining room, he looked wet. His favorite pastime was holding his breath. Pearl didn't know much more about him. She knew only from what she observed, which she found untrustworthy, and from what the children told her.

No one except the children ever told her anything and their theories were garbled, to say the least. There were so many children. Pearl felt it necessary to take into consideration, however, the fact that they grew rapidly and often wore different clothes so that there were undoubtedly not as many as there appeared.

There were just twelve of them. That was all. Not that that

wasn't enough. Many of the ones Pearl had first known here were gone now. Grown, they would go to the mainland to live and get jobs or go to school. Thomas was very generous. He paid for everything. The absent ones sent letters and remained devoted to him, but they were never encouraged to come back. Thomas' "family" remained prepubescent. So now Joe was the oldest here, and baby Angie the youngest. She had a withered leg. She had lovely blond curls and fat little cheeks and a poor withered leg. She went everywhere with the others though, carried along high on their shoulders, peeping and chortling to herself.

Pearl liked the pool. The bottom had been painted a very dark blue so that it looked as natural and bottomless as the sea. Anchored to its tiled lip was an iron bird. A work of art. Really worth quite a deal of money. There were a lot of objects around the place that looked valuable, even to Pearl's careless eye. The children crawled all over the thing, threw their bath towels on it, ate their lunch inside it. Pearl sometimes wished that she were smaller and could crawl around inside it too. She liked the twisted battered orbs that were its eyes, its empty iron spaces, the worm-eaten wood that made its legs and beak.

Pearl didn't swim but she liked to drink her cold white wine in the sunshine. Each morning she would empty half a dozen ice cube trays into a battered scotch cooler and work a half gallon of wine down among them and carry her burden out into the beginning day.

In the summer she limited herself to wine during the day for she thought that it enabled her to cope better with the children. Even so, she did not cope very well, although she did prefer conversations with them to bouts with the adults. Children were like drunkards really, determined to talk at great length and with great incoherence. Pearl more or less understood them in that regard.

Pearl let Tracker's little brother, Timmy, uncork her wine for her. He took away the cork for his gun.

"Pearl, Pearl, swim with us!" the children cried.

It was August, in the morning. The grass was yellow. Pearl's body shone with lotions and sweat.

"I won't swim," Pearl said languorously. "I'm not even willing to float." She laughed as they giggled at her.

"Pearl, Pearl!" the children called tirelessly. Through many seasons now, their voices had crooned to her, smoothly flying, silently and sweetly hunting her.

"Tell us a secret, Pearl."

She shook her head. "I have no secrets from you," she said.

Trip's lips brushed her ear. "Your chest looks funny, Pearl."

She opened her eyes. On her chest she felt something plump and moist. She looked at it rigidly. Just a fungus of some sort. Ripped from an oak. She flung it into the pool and closed her eyes again.

"Ugh," she said, "you and your games."

Trip had a birthmark on his face that Pearl did not like to notice. It was not disfiguring. It was more insulting than anything. He was perfectly capable of concealing it with make-up. Pearl knew that for a fact as sometimes it wasn't there on his cheekbone at all and he was just an ordinary good-looking boy. With a face appropriate to childhood, for isn't the face of childhood essentially the same everywhere? But Trip preferred to embellish the mark more than conceal it. It was about the size of a fifty cent piece and a brilliant raspberry color. It lent itself well to experimentation. Usually it appeared as a fox's head but sometimes its suggestions were more sexual. He was a walking ink blot. He was a rascal. He had always been a rascal. Years ago, the first year Pearl had been here, when they had sent him to Morgansport to school for the first time, he hadn't lasted out the day. Such an alert, smart child, charming in his new wool suit and his new sneakers and his brushed, bright hair. And he'd urinated over the other children's colors in art class. And he'd bitten the teacher who scolded him at nap time. He hadn't been in school since. Someone should have spanked him at the time, Pearl thought. They all needed to be spanked.

Pearl would never lay a hand on any of the children herself. Instead, she had developed a trick to take herself out of their range. True, the trick was unreliable, but when it worked it was wonderful. She concentrated, she rose in her mind, she moved of a distance. Her body would lie there, surrounded by the laughing children, but she would be gone. Beyond irritation or fright or boredom or knowing. Having knowledge without knowing, her thoughts far away, her body there, but in darkness, stroked by the whispers of summer. Her other self above. Coldly, cleanly empty of herself. Another thing. Miles up, miles out, needing nothing, gliding.

Every living thing suffers transfiguration. Yes, until the creation of Eve, Adam had fondled beasts.

"Come into the water now, Pearl," another child said.

"Oh I can't," she said smiling, "I'd drown." She smiled and smiled. She had risen like a saint, a stigmata of spilled wine upon her palms, leaving her body behind for them to worry as they wished.

She could sometimes will herself to be away for a long while. Sometimes, when she came back, she was not where she had been before. She was in a nightgown, in bed, her hair brushed out upon a pillow. She was at the supper table, dressed demurely in a dress that Thomas had ordered from a catalogue.

And Thomas would say in his unctuous, sexless voice, "You shouldn't spend so much time with the children. You should rest more."

When she and Thomas spoke to one another, it was principally about her health. He had not made life difficult for her here. He had never called her "loathsome." He took care of her actually. She lived in his house, ate his food, drank up his liquor. He was her guardian, her host. Even so, it was quite obvious to the children that there was pain between the two, and dislike. As with everything, they shaped this understanding to purposes that they approved of. There was nothing that the children would allow to pass without interpretation.

"Pearl," Thomas would say, "the children have their own rules. Their world is their own. You shouldn't try to enter their world."

"But I prefer their lives to ours," she would say.

Pearl always felt humiliated with Thomas. She didn't like to discuss the children's lives with him. Nevertheless, it was the case that Thomas had not made things difficult for her. He had not attempted to "take" Sam away from her. Sam was growing up in his own fashion. Things had settled down. Things were possibly even better. When Pearl approached Sam now, he did not strike out at her as he had when he was a baby. When he was a baby, Pearl had been covered with bruises. She could not hold him. He would not allow it.

"You must resist the children's ways, Pearl," Thomas would say. "You must make the effort. You're far too impressionable, you know. You allow them to take up too much of your time."

"I am on guard," Pearl would say.

She knew that the children were not what they seemed. She knew that many of the things that visited her in the long wasted hours of the day were not children at all. They were phantoms, aspects only of her fatuous, remorseful and destructive self.

Once Pearl had wanted death but since she had come back to the island she realized that death was a hopeless resolution at best. The soul separated from the body at last, yet still retaining memories and having hungers. That's the way she saw it. Yes. And what would be the use of it—to be dead yet still to have the hungers—the different hungers for love.

"Come in, Pearl, come into the water! We'll save you if you drown." She felt the small fingers laced in hers. She saw the children's soft hands with square pink nails, each nail holding a lovely crescent moon, a bit of the world reflected. Their wet heads dripped upon her breasts. There was a smell of dust, flowers, warm skin.

Jane was poking at an anthill by the side of the pool. She licked an ant off her finger and swallowed it.

"Please don't do that," Pearl said. "You'll get sick."

"They taste all right," Jane said. She was a stocky, tanned child, with small closely set eyes.

"Pearl, why do bees hum? Do you know, Pearl?" Timmy put his face up close to hers.

The sun held them all. Pearl didn't mind the daytime. It was dusk that made her unhappy here. The rest of the time she got by. But dusk was difficult for her. At dusk she switched to gin. Her marrying hour. The hour between the dog and the wolf. It sometimes seemed that dusk came to the island several times a day. Brought in by storms and fog. The change was in the fog. The Devil.

Pearl's mother had once told her that she must never be embarrassed to tell another that she had seen the Devil.

"Luther saw the Devil, Pearl, and Luther was a wonderful man. And he saw him in the bathroom. The Devil is everywhere, Pearl, and you must never be afraid to say you've seen him."

Her mother, bless her soul, was a little simple-minded, but in the long run it was all a matter of phrasing.

The children crept upon Pearl's lap and wrapped their arms around her neck.

"Don't cry, Pearl," they said, battering her with their soft wizard's paws. "It's a riddle."

Sometimes she felt that she had received innumerable and indescribable injuries from them.

"Look," Ashbel said. He was holding out a jar with two mantises in it. He had left his mudworks to do his share in pestering her. Ashbel was always building something. His little structures were scattered all over the island. Not far from the pool was his latest creation, a hummock of wood, grass and cardboard, which, he claimed, had three rooms. He would be a great architect, Pearl thought. Perhaps when he grows up he can build me a house just outside of heaven.

He smiled at her. But she did not want to look. What would she see? She looked instead toward the sea, her eyes catching on a shape, brown in the bright green of the bank sliding into the sea. It resembled an animal, big as a man, but on its side, heaving, its legs moving erratically, its muzzle snapping at the air. But it was nothing. A pile of mown grass that the boys hadn't taken to the flower bed yet. Nothing. A rotten dingy that the children played in. Nothing.

"Yes, look, Pearl," his twin, Franny, said, turning Pearl's face back to the jar with her hands. The children were so physical. Pearl felt unnatural in their embrace.

Ashbel flung the insects apart with a jiggle of his wrist. "It's a mommy and a daddy. It's a husband and a wife."

Pearl looked at the jar. The male mantis was scrambling up the glass side toward the lid, trying frantically to escape.

"Why did you want a baby, Pearl? Why did you want Sam?"

"Out of pride," Pearl said. "Women have babies out of pride," wondering if this might not be true.

"Joe says it takes between 2.9 and 3.2 seconds to make a baby, is that true Pearl?" Ashbel patted her hand with his, trying to get her attention.

"When little babies begin they have tails between their legs and gills in their necks, don't they, Pearl?" Franny said.

In the jar, one of the mantises was missing a leg and an eye. The creature was so graceful and such a pretty color but one of its eyes was dangling from its stalk and hanging like a bloody button.

"Ashbel," Pearl said. "I'm afraid your pets are quarreling or something."

"They're making love," the child said. "I let them do that."

"Your mother should cut your hair, Ashbel," Pearl said. The boy had beautiful, glossy thick hair, but really it was too long. He swept it back from his cheeks. It always seemed to Pearl that

Ashbel was grinning at her. He had two wonderfully new, white front teeth, slightly protuberant. Miriam should probably take him to a dentist as well.

Franny didn't resemble her twin. Her teeth looked almost gray. Perhaps she ate erasers or drank tea. Other than that, she was very pretty.

"Mother wouldn't notice about Ashbel's hair," Franny said. "Mother doesn't notice us from one day to the next." She tipped her head to one side, allowing her own shorter hair to fall against Pearl's cheek. "You're nicer than Mother," she said.

Children were quite disturbing really. It was difficult to think about children for long. They were all fickle little nihilists and one was forever being forced to protect oneself from their murderousness.

Pearl was distressed at her surly thoughts and straightened in her chair.

"I think your mother is very nice," Pearl said. "She has her work is all."

"Yes, she does," Franny agreed.

Miriam's skirts were taking up more and more of her time. People sent her material from everywhere. Each scrap had a meaning, each thread a karmic force. Pearl sympathized with her. No wonder she hadn't the time for the twins. Her mind was reeling with causality. She had the career of her food and the making of her cosmic skirts. Relating to her children wouldn't assist her much. And hadn't she related her heart out to her first-born? And hadn't that been to her confusion and sorrow? Buried beneath the rosemary now with a bag of marbles and a silver bunny cup. Perhaps, in her heart, Miriam felt the twins to be a little tasteless. Redundant. They were old enough not to have to depend upon a mother's enthusiasm for them. They could swim and knew the rules of the woods. They could make their own breakfast. They knew where the milk was and the extra blankets for the cold and the lamps for the dark.

"She is a very interesting woman," Pearl said.

"But she is not much fun to talk to," Franny said.

She lay her cheek against Pearl's head. "Your hair smells good," Franny said.

"I put a little honey in the shampoo," Pearl said. Children were friendly but they were decadent. And they kept changing the topics of conversations. Pearl tensed her shoulders and Franny raised her head, giggling.

"Our mother is no fun to talk to because every time you show her something you've done for the first time or tell her about something that's happened to you for the first time she just looks into one of her goddamned skirts and tells you that it's someone else's story." Franny said this loudly into Pearl's hair.

"Goddamn is not a nice word," Pearl said.

"All she ever talks about is the stuff in those skirts. She'll say, 'This piece of lace came from the baptismal gown of Remedios Borges, a young Spanish girl of the nineteenth century who died before she was ten and whose feces paintings were well received by the avant-garde aristocracy of Milan.'"

"Feces painting?" Pearl said faintly.

"The one I did," said Ashbel, "was of a house and a tree and a sun with spokes.

"I remember that," Franny said, wrinkling her nose. She was now at the stage where she was very hygienic. She was always washing her hands.

"I'm afraid you children are tiring me," Pearl said. Some of them were curled at her feet, stroking her ankles. She saw one urinating into a bush and another staring at her with the curious dispassionate waiting of a wild thing. Such children these with their condor eyes! Pearl felt her heart sink as she watched them.

Her eyes, averted now from the children, fell upon Ashbel's jar, where the male mantis was now disappearing at a disorienting rate. It was trying to mate with the female and it was actually succeeding although it now lacked both legs and a head. Where is the twins' father? Pearl thought in a panic.

"Where is your father?" she demanded.

"Oh, Pearl," Franny said, "you know he ran away."

"He started out after Miriam one day with a hatchet, thinking he was pruning a vine, and then he ran away," Peter volunteered.

"Do you remember the time I was playing with the lead soldiers on the porch and I had that wonderful battle plan worked out?" Ashbel asked his sister. "And mother came by and looked and tapped her belly button and said, 'This thread came from the jacket of a Confederate boy who was killed at the battle of Petersburg where the press of men was so great that the dead having no place to fall remained in the upright position.' Remember that?"

"I remember that," Franny said. "Mother and those awful skirts."

"Oh," Pearl said, "please go away." Children were so exhausting. And they were so close to her, breathing on her with their sweet breaths.

Then a boy said, "Yes, leave Pearl alone for a while."

"Who are you?" Pearl asked. "Now which one are you? Who is he?" she demanded of the others.

"Why that's Sam," Ashbel said. "That's your Sam!"

"Oh for godssakes," Pearl said irritably.

"Sam says he can make plants. Can he, Pearl?" Tracker said.

"Nobody can make plants."

"Pearl, you're so funny," Franny giggled.

Ashbel sniffed at Pearl's hair.

"If you mash up the pituitary glands of a cow and use it for shampoo would all the hairs on your head be able to see?" he asked.

"No," Pearl said brusquely. More children arrived by her chair with nothing to do. She hadn't the strength to get up and leave them. Certainly she would never have the strength to leave this island again. She would stay here forever, drinking herself dumb, all her wishes fulfilled.

For islands were the place for that sort of thing, were they not? The Fortunate Isles and so on. The place where children originate, the land to which the dead depart?

CHAPTER EIGHT

"What was the beast in *Beauty and the Beast*, Pearl? What did he look like?" Jane asked.

"I think he was supposed to be a snake," Pearl said.

"A snake! Yuk," Jane said.

Joe laughed. He was lying on his back, wearing a pair of tight black swimming trunks. He smelled like a sack of salt. He was very tanned. On Saturday night in Morgansport, the girls had to line their panties with Kleenex just at the thought of dancing with him.

Sometimes Pearl wondered if he wasn't a mutant or something, he was so marvelously hung. Perspiration popped out on her temples indicating the depth of her thoughts. She blushed. She had seen the rude and pragmatic way he flirted with the town girls. She could see one of them hoisted on an armrest in the movie theater's balcony, yipping and fluttering in the dark.

"You're pretty, Pearl," Timmy said in his growly little voice. "What are you thinking?"

Pearl's eyelids shook.

"There's a bug in your drink, Pearl, look," Jane said. "Do you want me to get it out for you?"

"I will drink around it," Pearl said.

"Why do you drink?" Tracker shouted, teasing. "Pearl! Pearl!"

"Because it makes your bones blossom, isn't that right, isn't that what you say Pearl?" Peter broke in eagerly. Peter wanted to be a magician. He thought such an act with bones would be the world's finest illusion. He pranced before Pearl in a torn up white sheet, sea signs scribbled on his skin with a felt-tip pen. She saw him twisting his fingers into talons and then back into fingers again.

"That's right," Pearl agreed. "I drink because it makes my bones blossom. That's what I say."

The children loved the image of it and could see the truth. They could see a fragrant branching tree of bones transformed into flowers. But when they kissed her they could taste only the unhappiness in which she dwelled. They could taste no sweet blossoms at all.

"Tell us a story, Sweet," Franny said suddenly.

"Yes," Tracker said. "Tell us the one about the island that was really a living creature."

"No," Franny said. "Not that one. Ashbel gets scared at that one."

There was an unknown island in the sea and lost people would find it, but whenever they tried to live upon it, it burrowed down into the sea and all the people were drowned, for it was a living creature and its feet were rooted in death.

Sweet changed it every time she told it. She fudged the point that the creature's feet were rooted in death.

"I can't think of any stories," Sweet said.

Sweet was getting too old for stories and games, thought Pearl. Her body was thinning out and her face was becoming angular and set. She was getting her own face and her own thoughts about things. She wanted to grow up and see the world as something simple and dangerous. She wanted to do something illicit.

Timmy's attention had been diverted toward his father who was walking, whistling, toward the sauna. Tracker, too, followed him with his eyes.

"Boys . . ." Pearl said nervously. It always made her nervous when they looked at Lincoln like that. They despised him. They were always thinking up terrible fates for him.

One of the small children gave Pearl a small tin pail full of blueberries. Seeing them made Pearl know she was hungry.

It must be almost noon, Pearl thought. Lincoln always whacked off in the sauna before lunch. She knew sometimes the boys spied on him.

Tracker was waving and smiling at Lincoln. Lincoln was too far away to hear the words Tracker's mouth was saying.

"Daddy, Daddy, you fuck, you creep, may spiders crawl up your ass . . ."

"Hush," she said. "Please hush." She put a blueberry in her mouth, then reached in the cooler and filled her glass again.

Joe was standing on his head. His legs were spread to their ultimate limit. Slowly, he brought them together again. He looked like some wildly exotic creature with swaddled testes between his shoulders.

"Lincoln starches himself in there, Pearl, we've seen him do it. There's a little hole in the wall behind the sumac. Come see, Pearl. We'll show you."

"No," Pearl said. She looked at them for a moment. "I'll get a rash from the sumac." She laughed. A wind blew through the trees and rustled them, making a sound like water boiling for tea.

Pearl kept the wine for a moment in her mouth without swallowing.

"He looks so goofy, Pearl. He sticks his tongue out. His eyes get wide enough to spit in."

"Why does he do that when he's got Mommy?" Jane asked.

"You don't have anyone, do you, Pearl?" Timmy said sadly. He moved his hands moodily through the blueberries without taking any.

"Pearl's got Walker," Jane said.

The littler children firmly believed that the dead were merely at the mercy of an implacable presence, more or less prolonged.

"Pearl's got us," Trip said. He had a sharp, sweaty smell. Once, on Christmas, he had given Pearl a pretty little glass jar with a silver cap, an old perfume jar. It had been filled with something that looked like blue Vaseline.

"It's a special ointment, Pearl," he had said. "Peter and I made it up especially for you. It's got thorn apple in it. You use it and you'll have wonderful dreams and won't need a man."

Pearl pursed her lips, remembering. She looked at Trip with her sun-blasted eyes, at his thin, rapid face. His happy tongue lolled.

"Do you think he could ever give himself a heart attack in there?" Tracker said hopefully. "It's so hot and he's so fat and all."

"I'd love to pull the kisser-button of my bow string back and kill him deader than Cock Robin," Timmy said.

"That's just a play bow you've got," Ashbel said. "It's like your pop gun. You couldn't kill anybody with it." He was bunched up at Pearl's knees. His lower lip sat primly behind his teeth.

"Once when I was showing my thing to Jane, and he caught me, he hit me so hard he knocked a tooth out," Tracker muttered.

"Who wanted to see your thing anyway?" Jane said.

"You shouldn't show your thing to the girls," Pearl said vaguely.

Joe was looking at her from his peculiar position, his muscular legs spread far apart again. He was looking at the level of the wine in the bottle on the grass. Joe was a bit of a prude as far as alcohol was concerned. He was a firm believer in the care and maintenance of one's own physical vehicle. Always running on the beach and doing hatha-yoga and this ridiculous thing on his head.

"You should try to cut down on your drinking," he said, upside down. "It's bad for the mind as well as the body. Each day some of the brain's neurons die and drinking simply speeds up the process. It's like a lot of little lights going out in your brain each day."

Everyone looked thoughtful. They looked at Pearl as though they could see her neurons going out right then, in style, light bulbs visible, snapping and cracking, exploding, fire-cracking and fizzle-shorting.

Pearl worked the bottle back into its melting nest of ice. She'd liked Joe better as a child when he'd been silent all the time.

"When men and ladies make babies do they lie down beside each other and hug and kiss each other first?" Franny asked, deftly changing the topic.

"Love is a secret thing, isn't it, Pearl?" Jane asked. She nuzzled Pearl's empty hand.

"Some kinds of love are hard to think about," Pearl admitted. To love was to immerse oneself in the waters of reality. She didn't know anything about it.

"We could slip some D-Con in his beer some night," Timmy said. He had curled his hands into fisty paws and was staring at them. "That might do it."

"Timmy!" Pearl yelled. "Stop that!" A thin band of chill encircled her forehead. "Lincoln is your father. He had a part in making you. Without him you wouldn't even be here."

Such a thought cinched the band of chill still more tightly above her eyes. The hot day rumbled with thunder although the sky was a perfect blue. The baby Angie babbled at her hip. Pearl looked. "Oh no, dear, I don't want that. Number Twos are not a nice thing to give to people. They are not a present, Angie. Pick me a flower or something. Franny, wash her hands. Put a diaper on her. She should be in a diaper."

Timmy was looking at Pearl darkly, as though he was going to cry.

"Daddy did not make me," he said.

"God made us," Tracker said.

Pearl looked at the group gathered around her. She looked at each of them in turn. She looked at Sam. Sam slept with his eyes open and watched with his eyes shut. She was sure of it.

"God made us," Tracker said again, satisfied. "That bastard didn't have anything to do with it."

Pearl stared at the sauna and imagined Lincoln tossing himself off in there, balls bouncing on the bench like peas in a pail. On his quest to conquer death by becoming father to himself.

Pearl rolled the empty glass against her cheek. Some of the children ran off to look through the peephole they had made. She could imagine what they saw—Lincoln with his head propped open on a smooth stone, an arm and leg dangling from a greasy shelf. Lincoln lying with his eyes closed, his lips half parted. His penis lying curled, a sweating snail. A muscle in his stomach twitching . . .

* * *

Lincoln rubbed his thumb across his chest, sloughing off a thin layer of skin. Gone. With its attendant angels. His mind was no more than meat, hanging strips of meat in his sweaty hair. He inched back slightly on the shelf so that his head hung backward. His eyelids fluttered. His cock rose. He made it swing. Probe the soupy air.

A pity a man so disciplined by nature should end up in this chaotic life. He really hated the island but here he was. With the women and the brats. With the smells of piss and pies and ironing. And that soul-less cold-assed bastard Thomas who paraded around like some exiled king.

Lincoln's cock fattened and grew sleek.

The pleasures of solitude, of unleashing the mind. Allowing it to wander off and penetrate the most preposterous hole. The dry and dusty fucks the women offered. That wasn't really for him. He preferred the pleasures the mind allowed. He had never much liked the idea of putting a portion of his body into a complementary part of woman. Key into lock. That sort of thing. Mighty mast into simple mast hole. It was so tedious. It was the mind that fucked the best. Consciousness doesn't mean shit.

These wretched children had an edge on him there. They were free from reason, utterly unself-conscious, utterly indecent. Civilization had rejected them. Not a one went to school. They were far too fine for school, Thomas said. Joe had gone for a while. He had played football and damned if he hadn't killed some kid. Lincoln had seen it from the bleachers with the rest of the family. Heard it more than saw it actually. Sound like icicles falling on a cement driveway. Little runt wearing an oversized helmet with a wolverine on it, and unfortunately carrying the ball.

Not a single person punished Joe for breaking the kid in half. Not one harsh word. Not even a protest from the runt's mother, who perhaps thought it better that her son died in young innocence than be a victim to life's later cruel delusions.

Joe had a tongue like a towel. Watching him eat was an amazing thing to see.

Lincoln cupped his balls. They were searing, they ached. He rubbed his hand up over his stomach, ring-a-rosied his yellow nipples, slipped onward to his throat, waggled his thumb in his mouth for a moment, licked the sweat from his lips.

The other children maddened Lincoln. Common little buggers. Possessing only a protean capacity for uninteresting change. Ions in the air they were. All dropped easily as cats. And they were worse than dogs. Noisy, fawning. Their human looks only kennels for dogs. He was still astonished that he had to be considered father to some of them. He loathed children. They had stomach aches, were stubborn and didn't flush the toilet. They shuddered at that which was not dreadful but were fearless about confronting physical realities that could wipe them out in a flash. Lincoln sometimes attempted to explain his feelings to them. They did not distress him intellectually (for after all they were just children) or physically (because they were well formed) or even ethically (for he tolerated their mild savageries). His dislike for them was *metaphysical*.

"Call me 'lovey,' Daddy," Jane had called to him each night as a toddler. "Say, 'Good night, lovey.'" The child then had been patient as stone and, like her mother, impervious to slight.

"Good night, lovey," Lincoln would repeat without tenderness, pulling her nightgown over her head, over her little sex, beardless as a bun, over her thin legs. In his children's presence, Lincoln was possessed by neither love nor guilt. In their presence, he was a balanced man.

He had been a balanced man before and he was a balanced man now. It was just in between where something terrible had happened, that something being Shelly's courtship of him. It had changed his life. Now he was here, a misogynist married, on an island full of children.

Once he had been a mathematician, a professor at a small university. He found his art, which depended upon the concept of nothing, congenial to his life in general. Numbers pure as light. An order in the universe. Three the masculine, four the feminine, seven the eyes of God. Shelly had been in one of his classes and he considered her to be the dumbest of the lot. She returned her papers blank. Only a few smudges and loops of hair to indicate the vast deserted regions of her brain. Lincoln was an arrogant and scornful man. He wielded words as a seal skinner does a club. The classroom was an arctic waste littered with battered puppy sensibilities. But Shelly refused to be intimidated. Her desire for him was inspired, unflagging and utterly sexual. She showed neither modesty nor common sense. She would not go away. Each night there were visitations and demands. She would enter his apartment in the guise of disorder, stinking of juices and dripping with sea water, staining his sheets and fouling his mind.

Lincoln's apartment was large and neat. He possessed only a few things but they were things that had been chosen with discrimination and taste. He did his own cooking in the small, well-appointed kitchen. He was always making perfect soufflés and flans and blintzes which he then dumped into the garbage for he worried about his health and weight. He didn't drink. He didn't dream. He took out few women, none of whom he touched. He didn't like their chests. He didn't like their odor for all they tried to hide it with the musk of bears and berries. Victims of the moon they were and easily deceived. Tits like doorbells. Eyes that widened with the hope of tears. They craved insult and abandonment, every one of them.

"Ignorant bitch," he'd say to Shelly as she moved around his rooms.

"Oh you're mean," she'd cheerily reply. "Your mother never laid you in the sun to give your heart its share of light."

"You're retarded," he would say.

At night, in bed, he'd clench his lips. He'd seal his ears. He concentrated upon the tiny blind and balanced man within himself. And he did not succumb, he did not falter. He endured like a monk, still with cold as she worked on him, as she kissed his every part. He was proud of his unresponsiveness. He would not be duped or managed.

Shelly had long black hair, down to her waist. Her pubis was a soft and mossy bank. It all made him sick. She would slip into the room while he was sleeping. He felt that she entered like a rat. He told her this. Wasn't the door locked? Had she no sense of herself? Weren't the windows sealed? Had she no pride?

She followed him everywhere, singing dirty jingles in his ear. She baked his bread, she pressed his shirts, she held his cock as he relieved himself. Actually he didn't mind the latter much. His piss made petals in the bowl. He gave a laugh. Unlike him. And turned the stream on her. It hit her belly with a smack like a snowball.

"I don't want you," he'd say with ragged breath as she flailed him with a cunt that fit him like a slipper. He could teach her nothing, not even the acceptance of his hatred. He had visions of murder, dismemberment, worse. He wished he had the courage and success of Claudius . . . to pour a poison in her ear, her eyes, to change her smooth body into a length of loathsome crust. He would sheer off her labia, make a broth, stuff a bird, have her help him eat it, on Thanksgiving Day. He would seize her throat with his jaws and worry it with joy until the bones broke like seeds on his teeth.

Yet how could he do any of these things? He was a civilized and realistic man. Until Shelly had entered his life and fixed him with her thirsty raven's maw, his days had been calm and ordered. He was at home in a world which he had made temperate by the sheer conviction of his personality. His ability to make others feel anxious, uncomfortable and ignorant confirmed the personal peace he felt which he considered unshatterable. He rose at seven, worked with weights, ate cold cereal and brushed his teeth with powders and strings. He took no salt or stimulants. He played tennis. He could converse on almost any topic. He had not traveled much but he had read extensively. At night his principal pleasure was to clamp earphones on his head and listen to Landowska.

Now he felt ruined. His mind was filled with dire and successful acts. He had exquisite visions of fucking Shelly's ass until it split like a peach.

Of course he was appalled at himself. At the university, his work began to slide. The numbers, the formulas he had loved for their beauty and worth deceived him. They caused him errors. They clumped across the blackboard like cows. He began to stammer. He said giddy things. He found his fly open. He took to staring at his students while they stared, baffled, back, and before his very eyes one day, a boy's head grew flat and slick and formed two ponds complete with ducks. Raised hands were cleavers for dividing him. A girl's mouth became a mare's wide and plushy slit.

Perhaps it was the weather. Perhaps Shelly was poisoning him in some way. Lincoln's heart pounded. His saliva tasted queer in his mouth. His tongue grew odors. He grew weak, sobbed daily, craved small comforts like a child. As he walked across the campus in the spring, his shoes black with the melting ground, Shelly would drift beside him like a fog, sickening his bones. He did not speak to her. He did not respond to her except in sleep, and then he woke up screaming, drenched in semen, dreaming it was blood. She was a witch, a poison woman, with weapons hidden inside her body. She was a bitch with a belly of ice to which his tongue stuck as though to freezing iron.

He feared sleeping. Even so, it seemed he dreamed while awake. It was spring. Small yellow flies hovered around his head. He walked and walked, trying to stay awake. It was a sunny town. Windows were draped in orange plastic to protect their items from the sun. Children ran before him laughing, their heads bleached out, holding dripping things to eat.

"Lincoln, sweetheart," Shelly said, "if you'd just come along with me, and be my husband and give me my family, you'd just be fine. You're just making yourself sick, sweetheart."

Lincoln stared at her aghast.

Lights burned day and night in his apartment and he took his rest sitting upright in a chair to avoid nightmares. The veins in his arms were discolored and his chest, his breathing, felt queerly light. What was the brine they'd packed the poet Byron in?

"I'm just loving you is all, Lincoln," Shelly said.

He feigned unconsciousness.

She fixed herself on his lap. She socketed his cock inside her with a sigh, and began to rock. In moments he had come. His shanks and hers were white. But he was still fixed fast. She rocked and rocked. She hugged him like clothing. The garment of Deianeira grafted to his skin. She put one little finger in his ass, one little finger in the corner of his mouth and her tongue in his ear. Her black rough hair fell against his nostrils and his eyes. All passages were blocked. He gasped, he choked, with effort he slipped free.

He wept with tiredness. He shook. He wanted a cup of milk. He wanted some clever conversation. He wanted to clamp his earphones on and hear the music of the spheres.

"I'm just a man," he said desperately, "and there's hardly anything left of me." He coughed. There seemed to be marbles sliding around in his chest. The apartment was a fetid cave. The breeze blowing through it seemed used up as though it had been blowing for years, over all continents and conditions of men, yet was still full of unpleasant surprises.

Lincoln returned to his chair and sat there unshaven, his jaw slack. His hair, which had once been so carefully groomed, was twisted in knots from Shelly's constant plucking at it. The chair contained his sweaty image. He fit it to a tee. A greasy imprint of buttocks, head and hands.

"You're the most nervous person I know," Shelly said from the bed, "but you're still the only one for me."

He looked at her, panting lightly. How had he come to this? A respectable man of forty. An effective, moderate and civilized man, never given to excesses. He could deduce nothing from this experience, this pursuit, this *mauling* except that he had been driven into hell. As an intelligent man, of course, he knew that there was neither heaven nor hell after death. So he was still, undoubtedly, numbered among the living. He was not dead, yet he felt pain and indignation as though his self were a dwelling that had been broken into and robbed. And rearranged. Which was worse.

He was not dead but he was cut off from life and health and ordinary pleasures. And all this by this girl, this cunt, this witch that rode his penis like a broomstick.

"Your love is a flogging," he said as calmly as he was able. A drop of spittle dangled from his chin. "It is a chamber of horrors. If you loved me, if you had any capacity at all for love, you'd see I was miserable, sick, perhaps even dying and you would go away."

"Oh, sweetheart," Shelly said, "we can't part now. You're about to be a daddy in a month or so."

"A daddy," he repeated, grinning like a skull.

"Yes, yes," she laughed. She bounced from the bed and ran into the bathroom. Her stomach *did* look slightly distended as though she'd just had a feed. When she returned, she was fully dressed. She had brushed her hair and tied it back with one of Lincoln's ascots.

"That is impossible," he said, still grinning.

"Oh sweetheart," Shelly said. "I've been faithful to you. As you know, I've scarcely spent a second from your side."

"I'm sterile," he said. "Sterile as a stick."

"Now that's just not true," she said. "You've already started a lovely big baby."

"You're a simpleton," Lincoln said. "You are ignorant of medical fact. I have no sperm. Or rather, there are spermatozoa but they are immature. They lack mobility."

"Is that right?" Shelly murmured. She was making the bed and tidying up the apartment, something Lincoln had never seen her do before. He looked at her warily.

"After the baby's born, we'll go to my home," Shelly said. "You'll like it there. It has a pool and a tennis court."

Lincoln pointed a trembling finger at her belly. "Whatever you're breeding in there has nothing to do with me! You are a carnal, careless woman. Many of your men friends on campus could have made that, but I did not."

"You're making such a fuss over one little sperm, Lincoln. It's not like you to be so misguided. It just takes one determined little sperm."

"I do not have determined little sperm," he said. "It's a sign of high I. Q." He chuckled weakly. An educated member! The things it wouldn't do ...

"Imagine the journey, Lincoln," She said. She clasped her hands together fishlike and swam through the air. "The dangers. The attrition."

"Attrition!" Lincoln said, surprised.

"A woman's greatest secret is her emptiness, as you know, Lincoln, but in that emptiness is the shadow. Out of millions, thousands reach the gate but then only one is chosen by the shadow. And then the way is closed."

"Perhaps it's a cold," Lincoln said. "Or sometimes cancer will bloat a woman."

". . . the way is closed. The barricades go up. The other hopefuls hesitate and die." Shelly folded her hands on her stomach.

"It's just fucking," Lincoln said. "And then it's enzymatic action."

"The precise nature of the blocks remains unknown. But one enters. It is only one which is acceptable to the surface of the emptiness. If others entered, life would not occur. Something else would occur."

Lincoln looked at her feverishly. His face was burning, his eyes were burning. Polyspermy. Is that what she was referring to? Nonviable. Such a muddle-headed girl. Tells the truth but wrongly. Making fancies out of fact. Her mind, a snare. But polyspermy! She had the gist of it. With it, reproduction of a species would not occur sexually. His sterility was not nothing then? Reversibility proves validity? Not nothing, the absence? His mind recoiled, then pitched forward.

". . . the child begins," Shelly was saying. "At first it resembles a signet ring."

"There is no child," he said desperately.

"Babies come because it's their time to come."

"I have no more interest in straightening out your confusions. I take no responsibility for your condition. I am not the father."

With effort he rose from the chair. He did not know his purpose in doing this, but it seemed necessary that he rouse himself. Leaning his forehead on the wall, he pulled on a pair of trousers. They hung loosely on his hips. He was surprised at his thinness. He felt there was no more to him than the heaviness of his breath. Perhaps a lung had collapsed. He should get to the hospital, call a cab, get to the hospital, cancel the lease on the apartment, get some rest, allow no visitors.

"I need something to eat," he said. "Please fix me something to eat." He went into the kitchen. The cupboards were bare. Nevertheless, there was a bad smell. He opened the refrigerator.

"The milk's soured," he said. "Everything's wrong. I used to have proper meals. You've ruined my life. When did I last eat?"

Was it summer? Was it spring?

He fell straight forward on the floor, fracturing his nose and knocking himself out.

Lincoln spent six weeks in the hospital. Bed to bath and back again. Serenity. Juices. Pressed sheets. There was no word from Shelly. The doctors came by each afternoon at four except on Sundays when a clergyman appeared. The clergy spoke of odds and pieces and read the news aloud as though Lincoln, in his disorder, had been struck blind. The clergy was jolly and cursed a lot.

"There's a chicle shortage," he said, "and now they're putting plastic in our gum." He shuffled the pages. "Do you chew? Not you? . . . Well, in Portugal, a woman confessed to murdering twenty-six people over a period of ten years. In Florida, a man was arrested for surf-casting for sharks off a bathing beach." He shook his freckled head and swore. "I've always admired those fish myself," he said. "They don't lie sleepless in the dark and weep for their wickedness. There's a moral beauty there."

Lincoln agreed to just about everything. He felt in a holiday mood. What difference did words make anyway? Or one's behavior in the world? His scornfulness left him. He had been sick, the victim of chills and fantasies, and now his only ambition was to get well. He had no plans and was reluctant to leave the hospital but one could not be the guest of pneumonia forever. He had a little money. He would travel someplace. He would tutor. He would live a modest life, generous to himself. A chop at eight. And in their seasons, artichokes and oysters. A paperback collection. Perhaps on Sunday, a drive to some scenic overlook. He couldn't think of what to do actually. He felt a little worn. A loaf of bread slightly sampled. The life that was left to him taking the curve of Shelly's mouth. The life that was gone the shape of her hunger as well. His cock stood up beneath the sheets, inappropriate to his attitudes.

The clergyman's freckled skull shone through his thinning hair. What was it that happened to redheads when they died? Unlucky. Became beetles. Even so, the man loved his jokes. He rolled back his jaws with laughing but didn't make a sound. The lions didn't eat Daniel because they didn't know how good he was. Ha. There was no money in the chaplaincy. He wasn't a bad sort. At night he guarded bridges for the state, a way of keeping body and soul together. He spent a lot of time with Lincoln because, as he told him, Lincoln was basically a healthy man. The terminal cases made him nervous. Caused his nose to run.

Lincoln had no other visitors. Shelly never arrived. He kept expecting to see her at the door, hysterical, overweight and over-wrought, demanding money and marriage. This would have given him cause for righteous scorn. He felt that if he could see her one more time he could excise her from his life and mind forever. Her absence, however, exerted a very strong influence. Face to face he could banish her. But she did not present herself. When he'd fuck her bottom, had it been her face he'd seen? He was puzzled, then annoyed. Then he grew concerned. He felt his emotions manipulated, as though he were following steps in a manual. Nevertheless, she could be dead, in his apartment, right at that moment, and he would be responsible. Lying, leaking, as potatoes do when gone, with a terrible smell. Shelly dead, behind a locked door, with the lease paid in full for a year. For that was the sort of man that Lincoln had been. Solvent. A wonderful risk.

And now he was responsible.

For signs of omission as well as emission. Ha.

He requested tests to be run on his ability to father children. "I have been falsely accused," he told the doctor. A nurse arrived and milked him briskly for a sample, and the next morning he was taken to a small office to hear the results. There was a diagram of the prostate on one wall. On the other was a colored photograph of a covered bridge in Vermont. Lincoln sat in a very uncomfortable vinyl chair to which the backs of his legs periodically stuck.

"I want the results of this for the courts if necessary," Lincoln said to the doctor.

"Very well," she said, "but the answers are all on the palm of your hand."

Lincoln looked quickly at his hands. Did she think he fiddled with himself? Had something taken root? Bulbs? Or was there a sign, easily read, on the flesh of the barren men? A broken circle, proved perhaps by science?

His hands were slim and rather ruddy.

"Look here," the doctor said, pointing to the wrinkles encircling the very tops of his wrist. "These lines. They're called bracelets. When they go up in a curve, right into the heel of your hand, they indicate, oh shall we say, reproductive problems. But that's not your case at all. Your bracelets don't enter the palm."

Lincoln looked at her dumbfounded. The hospital was supposed to have the finest minds and research facilities in the Northeast. Yesterday, his semen was whipped around in a twentieth-century centrifuge, and today he was victim to this stupid dialogue. There was several million dollars worth of laboratory equipment here and he was trying to keep up his end of a conversation with a shaman.

"What sort of a professional are you, for godsakes?" Lincoln said.

"Oh, reading palms is just a hobby. Life lines, love lines, Mars and Fate lines. It's astonishing how it all proves out. Were you aware that nothing is more clearly indicated in the palm than insanity? But I just dabble in this for the relaxation. It's like reading mysteries. I just offer this to you for what it's worth."

"Well it's certainly not worth much," Lincoln said moodily.

"Here we go then," the doctor said, and slid out an eight-by-ten photograph from a filing drawer. "This is a scanning electron micrograph. It's been enlarged some four thousand diameters."

Lincoln looked. It seemed a picture taken from a planetarium. Flashy rockets with fat whip tales against a black backdrop of sky. There were a considerable number of them.

"The sperm is removed from the semen by centrifugation and shadowed with platinum." The doctor pointed with a scrubbed nail to the slightly conical, cottony head of one of the things in the photograph. "The sperm head consists of densely packed chromatin, the hereditary material, covered by the acrosomal cap covering the enzymes that accomplish the penetration of the egg. Behind the head is a short segment containing mitochondria that supply energy to power the long flagellum."

"I can't believe this," Lincoln said.

"I have no reason for deceiving you," the doctor said.

"This is a joke!"

The doctor laughed.

"Shit," Lincoln had said.

When he had been released and gone back to his apartment, Shelly was there waiting for him with a little bundle of meanness. There didn't seem much he could do about it. He was a man without a future. He had come to the island then and here he had stayed.

* * *

In the sauna, Lincoln's cock slipped shriveled from his hand. Thinking about Shelly always depressed him. He wasn't concentrating. He began to pull angrily but then settled down to caring for himself as only he knew how. He pulled and stroked it, pinched it dearly, snuggled and slapped it, made it sway like a snake, charmed. He had a pleasurable ripple of anticipation. He arched his body just a little bit, slowing it down.

Who was the Nazi who bit the jugular of the boys he buggered?

Who was Tiresias that he was so lucky?

Lincoln's tongue clicked against his teeth.

Really, man cannot bear too much reality. And if man cannot, then what can but the insensate? Best to forget the past. There aren't the words for half of what goes on in this life. And where's the life gone that's lost in the living, as the poet asks ... Shoot your wad at that ...

His stomach bloated. He pounded his cock against it, against his belly puffed out with fancies and ultimate dreads. He grazed the side of his cock with one finger and rolled it lightly around the strained foreskin. His breast heaved. He bucked. A spume of come struck him lightly in the face.

Lincoln lay panting, his eyes shut. He felt a disemboweled and sacrificial thing, on a mountaintop near the sun, in the days when the belly's pleasure fed the soul.

He groaned. His eyes rolled and then focused as he pulled himself up to a sitting position. His heart pounded in his fatty chest. He could hear the slight hiss of steam in the room.

He lowered himself to the floor and stepped into the shower stall, turning on the water full force. He felt vague shocks rippling across his back and down his arms. He leaned against the wooden, curtainless cubicle. His heart sounded like the banging of some enormous, malfunctioning engine. The water moved sluggishly down the drain. He turned off the water abruptly and reached for a towel. His clothes were folded neatly on a bench. He dried himself and reached for his Jockey shorts. He heard a sound at the back of his head and slipped awkwardly on the wet floor at the sound, dragging his clothes with him. His skin tingled. His mouth formed the names of his children. The names were on his lips like bubbles of spit. One stone settled against another in the grate ...

* * *

"What's that?" Pearl said sharply.

"You've dropped you glass, Pearl. Look, it didn't break." Peter retrieved it for her politely, wiping it out with the hem of his sheet.

Lincoln opened the door of the sauna and walked into the meadow. Pearl was relieved to see him.

"Hello, Daddy," Jane bawled.

Lincoln responded with a cursory flap of his hand.

He was empty again, Pearl supposed. Ready to be filled with the sight of the way things seemed again, she supposed.

Tracker was feigning jabs at his small sister. He had a long body but short legs. "Daddy, Daddy," he mimicked. "You don't know anything, Jane."

Peter said, "I bet I know something that nobody here knows. I bet nobody here knows what it was they did first to make mummies in Egypt."

"Mommies?" Jesse looked interested.

"They took their brains out through their noses," Peter said grandly.

"Echhh," Franny wailed.

Disgusted, Jesse dove to the bottom of the pool. Pearl saw him lying down there on his stomach. He would stay down there, it seemed to Pearl, for incredible lengths of time. He said it was easy. He said all you had to do was close your nose and ears.

"I know something you don't know," Joe said lazily to Tracker. He was lying down now on his back, squinting at the younger boy. "Someday there's going to be a girl who wants to put your pecker in her mouth."

Tracker's eyes widened. He was horrified at the thought.

"You're all so dumb and silly," scolded Sweet. "Honestly, you make me sick." Her auburn hair shone prettily in the sun. She held Angie in her arms and turned around and around with her.

"What's that, Sweet?" Franny asked in a high, cautious voice.

"What's that that's wrong with you?

"Nothing's wrong with me," Sweet snapped. "You're the ones who are dopes. Little kid dopes."

"No, you've hurt yourself. You've cut yourself. You've got blood all over your bottom."

The children looked at her from a great distance.

"Oh, Sweet," Pearl said, "come here, dear . . ."

Sweet brushed the palm of one hand across the back of her flowered bikini. It was soaked with menstrual blood. She hurriedly placed Angie on the grass and moved off toward the house in a graceful, frightened lope.

"What happened to her?" Jane said, worried. "What hurt her?" She moved her thumb wildly in her mouth.

"When girls change into women, they bleed," Joe said. "And they bleed once a month like that unless they're making a baby and then they don't bleed."

Pearl threw an ice cube in her glass and poured wine after it. The children had eaten all the blueberries.

"Do you want some of my pear, Pearl?" Ashbel said. He had split the pear in two. Even the seeds were halved. Pearl saw the teeth marks in the fruit's white meat. Being a child is living in a world apart, she thought. A world all sufficient unto itself, and when one falls from it, it is like an angel cast from heaven. Magic envelops you as a child but then the magic vanishes . . . poor Sweet, she thought.

Pearl herself had not menstruated in over a year. It was the drinking, she supposed. The drinking had made her unattendant to a normal moon.

CHAPTER NINE

Pearl pinched a tick between her fingernails and dropped it on the grass. She ruffled the hair lightly with her fingers to seek out another. Awful things . . . they'd get into an animal's coat, burrow right beneath the skin sometimes and fester there. As a child she had been dedicated to their extinction. She had a jar of kerosene beside the porch steps and she would drop them in there. They were worse in the poor dog's ears and around his eyes . . .

"Ouch!" Tracker yelped. "That hurt, Pearl."

Pearl held a tick with a flake of skin still clenched between its jaws. Tracker was rubbing his neck.

"Well you have to get them out," Pearl said. "You can get sick from them." She pinched it between her nails. It made a tiny snap.

"Crazy Pearl, nice Pearl," Tracker said. He rolled out of her reach and sat rocking on his heels in the grass. Beside him sat Sam. They had been born within days of one another. Tracker was intelligent but rough and greedy. Sam was . . . Pearl didn't know what Sam was. He looked at her from his impassive eyes. His eyes were curious. The irises appeared oval-shaped. With shame, she knew she was afraid of him. He seemed all the disorder of her heart. She saw the infant in his face still. His other face, his boy's face, was harder for her to recognize. He didn't speak to her as the other children did. He kept away. She had no real sense of his purposes. Were not his purposes rooted in her responsibility? But she was an irresponsible woman, removed from everything, floating through space, exorcising longing. She would have liked to speak to him more, tuck him in his bed at night, share the night with him in her room. She did not want to be alone. Even wild animals don't sleep alone. It's too dangerous. Even a dog discovers in the darkness things invisible to men. In the night, demons chattered in her aching head. Not voices at all but comprehensible all the same. Terrible things. Creeping or winged, dark and avenging, carving a woman like her but different, out of carrion, out of mold. Carving this woman out with their sharp beaks. It was the drinking that caused the apparitions, Thomas told her, but if this were true, and Pearl did not concede to Thomas that it was, it was also only the drinking that could protect her from them.

Everything depressed her. Thomas would say, as though to reassure her, that she was not at all well. Tears rolled down her cheeks, bringing the flavor of tanning lotion to her lips. Oh the idea of the infinite is always present, the marvelous is so near, and then one gets bogged down in the arbitrariness of life. It is all hopeless. Absurd. She was not well, but she had been sicker before. A crisis had passed. And something wrong had been set right. But there was something else, something monstrous in that rightness. And that was what she wanted to remember. Did she not drink to remember it?

She suspected that she was maudlin. In soberer moments, she was quite aware of this. And yet even though her suffering was foolish and misplaced, her life had become an agony with it, and if what she felt now was the disproportionate anguish of the drunk, it was anguish after all, and it was overwhelming.

An ant crawling across her hand made her skin tickle. She looked down and pressed her thumb upon it the same instant that a bluejay screamed close by. She jumped, surprised.

"It's all right," Sam said, his eyes widening, "don't cry."

"You love me, don't you, Sam?" Pearl looked past him toward the house. She wished it were time for a real drink. The children's shadows were growing upon the grass.

"You have to love someone, Sam," she said after a moment.

"I love you," he said.

But it was not true, she knew. Pearl looked at the infant's face framed by the shaggy, sun-bleached hair. He was shirtless and wore new but muddy denims. He sat, fixed in sunshine, smiling. She took a swallow of wine. He knew her fearful thoughts of him. No one who has private thoughts going on in his own head is quite sure of their not being overheard. Any child knows that. Sam understood her thoughts. Was not his understanding reflected in the oval irises of those eyes? She wished she did not have those thoughts. She drank to get beyond them. She drank in the hope that her drunkenness would produce a clarity that would usher her into effective love. She drank because sometimes she felt her whole body gleaming with it. And whatever she wanted to see, she could see.

One of the children farted.

"That was Tracker," yelped Franny. "Tracker let the Devil out!"

Tracker leapt up, his arms flailing, but Franny danced nimbly out of his range. She was a humorous, coquettish child. She did a cartwheel out of sheer, mocking joy.

Tracker took several steps after her, but it was a movement apparently without threat, for he squatted on the ground abruptly and assumed a peaceful, far-away look. It was as though a gate had suddenly swung shut upon him. A gate, a wall of boards, protecting him from pain and confusion. He flopped on his back in the grass.

Tracker was rowdy and probably cruel, but what could Pearl do about that? Sam was an ever-increasing influence on all of them but what could Pearl do about that? She herself was a weak and evil woman. She was evil because she was unbalanced, she mistook appearance for reality, and she was empty as a sucked egg.

She worked the bottle up from the ice and filled her glass again.

Timmy and Jane were crawling around inside the sculpture at the edge of the pool. Jesse was still under water.

"Be careful around that thing's head," Pearl called. The year before the bees had made honey but it had been bad honey, poisoned really, because it had been made from rhododendron blossoms. Timmy had eaten some and gotten sick.

"We are not playing around its head, we are playing where it pisses," Timmy said.

"What was it like when Sam lived inside of you?" Jane asked Pearl. "Did it feel funny? The little hole that ladies have . . . is that where the souls of babies live?"

"Tell us a story, Pearl," said Franny. "Tell us the one about the king and queen who couldn't have children until the old woman told the king to catch a fish with golden wings and clean it and cook it and give it to the queen to eat and the king did," Franny said. Her face was bright with expectation. She sat, cradling Angie in her lap, squeezing the baby half blue in her enthusiasm. Sometimes she quite forgot that Angie was not a doll. Angie gave a squeak. Franny looked at her, surprised, and let her crawl off into the flowers.

"The king did," Franny went on, "and he gave it to the cooks to wash it and clean it and fry it and serve it to the queen and the cooks did, they washed it and cleaned it and threw all the inside stuff . . ."

"Entrails," Ashbel said.

"Ohh," Pearl sighed.

". . . out the window where the cow ate them and later the cow and the queen both had babies on the same day and the cow had a human baby and the queen had a baby that was just like a cow's baby . . ."

"So now you've told it all yourself," Jane said irritably from within the sculpture. She looked at her thumb, which looked wonderful. She thrust it into her mouth. Her eyes glazed.

"Let's go to the stone house," Timmy said, "and tell a story there."

Pearl couldn't hold the children in her mind anymore. She couldn't keep their features distinct. They were silent now around her.

The stone house. She had never entered it herself but the children talked about it often. The degree of their captivity in their childhood amazed her. Even Joe and Sweet were reluctant to leave the rituals of that childhood . . . the secret society of childhood from which banishment was the beginning of death. Joe and Sweet, Trip and Peter, along with the others, the littler ones, heeded the story they had made down there. Sam's story really. Sam's formulation of their world suited them.

The day seemed colder. Pearl pulled a shirt over her bikini. The sun was sliding down in the sky.

Sam was not yet seven. His birthday was tomorrow. "Speedily a tale is spun, with much less speed a deed is done . . ." It was as though he had grown by one of the devices of his story. He grew by the hour as other boys grew by the year. In one hour he seemed as others were in one year . . .

Pearl pulled her shirt around her more tightly and rested her chin on her chest. She smelled the scorched grass and the children's sweat and her own. I have to have a real drink soon so I will not become confused, Pearl thought. The time had passed. One sits down to a glass of wine and the years pass. Nothing magical about that. It had taken Sam almost seven years to become almost seven. And she had been with him all the while.

And yet she did not know him. She saw in his face only the face of that fierce dark infant who had torn her breast. Since that day she knew she could not love him as she might. Love for Sam would entail accepting the monstrosity of salvation. The others were unafraid of such salvation. They were children. Their world was as the world would be. Once, in the very earliest time, a human being could become an animal if he wanted to and an animal could become a human being. There was no difference. That was the way it was.

"Come on, come on," a child cried.

Sam shook his head.

Once the stone building had been a slaughterhouse. Blood had beaded in the dust. A smoky fire burned outside to keep the flies away. Then briefly it had been a chapel. And then a greenhouse. And now it was theirs. They lit candles and played in the dark with Aaron's animals.

Thomas knew the children used it but he didn't know what they did. There are fewer experiences for the body than for the mind, Thomas would say. It is through the mind that the human mud can be turned into spirit. Thomas allowed the children their privacy in the stone house. Their life on the island, superficially so chaotic, was actually quite structured, except for the summer months when they were allowed the holidays of ordinary children.

But in the winter, long hours of each day were set aside by Thomas for instruction, whether it be physics or reading or astronomy. He liked to keep his hand upon them all, but he would be the first to say that the cultivation of the spiritual self was more important than formal education. This cultivation, this discovery, he allowed them to make for themselves, believing that, as children, their imaginations were far more intricate and honorable than his own. Show me your thoughts when you are ready, Thomas would say. He believed in the necessity of secrets. He believed in the children. And he allowed them the secrets they kept from him in the stone house.

But the children kept no secrets from Pearl. She knew what they did there. Her world and theirs were very close. It was as though she were present, always, with them.

In the summer it was cool, almost cold. Half the floor was earth, the other half, planks laid over earth. The walls were stone except for the south wall, which was of small panes of glass, put in when part of the building had been converted into a greenhouse. Hot-water pipes ran along the ceiling. Scraggly plants grew from collapsed seedling boxes. Other, dried, plants hung down from hooks, their bulbs flayed and strangely healthy-looking. The room slanted back and telescoped into a smaller, empty room. The entire house was empty of furniture except for a long pine table against the north wall. On this table were the carvings that had been on the library mantel when Pearl had first come to the island. Twelve small figures, dry and light with age.

Each child took the carving that was his and settled down with it in the place that was his and they would wait. They would wait for their shadows to come to them. Their other, stronger, and more magical selves.

Sam had shown them how to do this. He had never spoken about it. He had just shown them.

Many times the shadows didn't come. The children would not admit to this if it were the case. It was hard for them to distinguish between the real shadow and something that they had just made up in their urge to exhaust the darkness here, something created out of air, no more separate from them than the real face is from the reflected image.

In the beginning the children would come down here to tell stories and scare one another. It was like the beginning of the world, full of chaos and warring seeds. The stories would get all jumbled up and the children would shriek and quarrel with excitement and disgust.

Trip had told Miriam's little Johnny such a bad story once that Johnny had died. Trip wouldn't say what it was. He had been younger than Johnny at the time. He had just been showing off. After Johnny died, Trip had been mildly shocked by handling a worn plug in space heater and after that he could no longer remember the story he had told.

Trip decided not to tell stories anymore but to stick more or less to the facts. Trip's interests now were electromagnetic wave propagation and creating an android out of scrap metal like Doctor Universalis.

In the stone house now there was only one story that was told. The story of Aaron and Emma. The children never tired of it. Children who were gone, who had left the island long ago, who were adults now, had had a part in the making of it. For years it had not been finished. But now with Sam, it was close to completion. The circle was closing.

The sun bored through Pearl's closed lids. Not just one circle, but two, closed and intersecting, the union of two worlds.

The children sat on the cold earth floor, in their darkness, in that tremendous human darkness that they were aware of only when they were still, when they tried to conjure up the dream and couldn't, the time before the shadows of the stories came. They sat waiting, sighing a little, holding the worn little objects that Aaron had made in his fear. Holding them, eyes shut, seeing with their minds, inching out little by little from that tremendous human darkness . . .

What a story it was. A story that fit them all so perfectly. A story that could be refined each day to their changing sensibilities.

Emma's first child's name was Stark. All twelve had names and natures but Stark seemed the best, the most impossible and pronounced, because he was the first.

Zezolla was the last. Still a baby when Aaron died. Franny sang a song for Zezolla.

> ". . . she had a wart in the middle of her chin
>   she called it a dimple but a dimple goes in . . ."

When she sang the song to Angie, Angie would laugh. The baby did have a dimple in her chin, but hers was a very pretty one.

The children held their animals up to their faces and felt the hollows that were their eyes. They put the animals in their minds. They were children here, making believe. Outside, the August day was burning down with its dry salt heat, but inside the children shivered as the animals that Aaron had skinned long ago shivered. They shivered and cried in their skinlessness, their otherness. Sam told them this.

Somewhere is your animal, and it is important that you know him, that you know how to reach him, or you will be nothing. You will always be afraid. You will have nowhere to rest and be safe.

They had been coming down here each day this summer. And as Aaron made the carvings and Emma had made her children, so these children made their story, the story becoming daily more and more a living thing they could almost touch, a large fantastic butterfly, flying among them, a butterfly looking like a dark hand with outspread fingers gathering them together.

* * *

The first building that Aaron had made on the island was this stone house. He'd lived here with the meat he'd made. For this was where he'd salted the animals when he had been a trapper, flayed and stretched them, cored their brains. Sometimes he would begin to eat them when they were still alive. A chthonic act, appropriate in this partially subterranean place, this murky grotto.

Aaron was a savage here. Blood beneath his nails. Blood upon his boots. A preposterous and inconsistent youth, all dark ignorance and strength. He could skin an animal so perfectly you couldn't see the fault ... moving his knife around the hind foot, slitting the skin along the back of the leg to the base of the tail, carefully around the tail, down the other leg, skinning out the feet, keeping the nails. Then peeling it off. Just as easy. Like an orange. Detaching the head, cleaning it out with a stick and some water . . .

Even today, in the heat of the summer, the children could almost smell the cooling blood and hot dust. They could imagine his heavy blotched hands carving and dividing, skinning a thing that hung by the heels, a thing turning and turning, catching the light, the sorrel hairs tipped with gold that glistened . . .

How clearly the children could see this. How vividly, in their minds, the things swung; so vivid in their whiteness, in their nothingness. Their skins, their outerness, their otherness lying apart . . .

Aaron could skin a bear cub in a minute and a half.

Aaron could empty and mount an animal so brilliantly that it would seem whole, uninjured, as though a puff of breath in its cold nostrils would set it to running again. There had been so many of them, those animals, those things that had been snared or shot or poisoned or drowned, with no forgiveness asked nor blessing bestowed.

Aaron prided himself on his agility. There wasn't anything he couldn't track or trap. He could catch a songbird with his hands and break its heart with his thumb. With the animals in traps, the ones with the fancy coats, he wouldn't shoot them and muddle their coats. He'd stomp on their hearts with the heel of his boot. He'd always know where its heart was and he'd stomp it there. It would never seem too painful. It would just break the creature's heart.

But trapping lost its crude charm and Aaron killed just for sport for a while. He liked the bow and arrow best. It was so economical and silent. He liked the silence of it. He could shoot an arrow three hundred yards. Like a Turk. The flight of an arrow is a terrible thing. It can be seen and not avoided.

The last animal that Aaron killed spoke to him as it was dying, and its blood did not run red as an animal's blood. It was sad but it was mad too and it spoke to Aaron, although not in words, and Aaron understood it. He wasn't frightened. He laughed at it. It was no more than a carcass with flies upon its teeth and he was a live man. He laughed at himself too for living alone so long in the wilderness that such a thing would happen to him. He decided to make his mark on civilization for a while, make some money, travel and learn. He came out of the wilderness. He left his guns to rust and his bows to warp. He turned his energies to society, and everything he fancied he took.

By the time he was thirty-five, he was worth several hundred thousand dollars. He read Latin and he had danced with princesses. He was in Europe when he met Emma.

And Emma, as the children had long ago established, was a witch.

She hated salt. She vomited needles. Her witchcraft looked like a piece of red chalk, but Aaron didn't care. He was full of himself and he didn't care at all about anything. He picked up the piece of red chalk and put it in his pocket, and then he had to follow her around. There wasn't anything he could do about it. After having been lucky for all that time, he was now as unlucky as a fox fallen down a well.

Emma put her witchcraft in him and made him need her. She wasn't pretty and she wasn't rich and she certainly didn't have nice ways. She didn't think much of Aaron's learning. "Fuck Ovid," she would say. She never had a mother. She was born of something horrible. A kidney frying and splattering in a pan. Her arms and legs were always scratched up and her skin was burned dark from the sun and her hair was matted, falling over her shoulders and hanging down into her eyes. But none of the ways she looked mattered because she made Aaron see her as she fancied. She had witched him that way. Emma did her witching poison by staring into the mirror at herself until the mirror got all discolored and greasy, and then she took the grease and put it in the food.

The children had her picture, which just showed how clever she had been. The children knew enough not to be deceived by a photograph which showed her pretty much like the other women of their time, and even as Pearl looked today ... skinny and sad, her dark hair pulled carelessly back, her eyes puzzled and bereft, the structure of her bones reciting in its witch way, the image of any other baby-raising mother of the century before. The picture was her witchcraft too, just like the piece of red chalk. It had survived all these years so the children could have it now, so they could know and appreciate her cunning.

Emma made Aaron marry her, and she made him forget all of his wandering ways and all of his intellectual pride. She made him take her back to the island, the place he had begun and abandoned so many years before he'd come across her. And there, on the island, in the wilderness once more, there were twelve years of silence, of waiting.

Emma made him build her a big house, big but not too fine, with many rooms. And other buildings, boathouses, and barns ... She made him obsessed with building and filling up the place. Furnishing it as though for a huge family, as though for important guests. But there was no family and no one ever came to visit them, just the boats and that brought the lumber and the tools, and the fine furniture and valuable art. Aaron just kept building and filling the rooms with circumstance and detail and Emma kept filling it with her emptiness. It went on for years like this, with nothing but the loneliness between them. The childishness and loneliness Emma wore in her magic like a second skin.

Aaron did everything she asked, for she had an enchanted will. And with her will she made him accept the animals she began to gather around her to gnaw at her loneliness. Aaron collected some of the animals, alive now, to be her companions. Living ... their hearts pounding blood not dust. Half-tamed or not tamed at all. How his life had changed! For Aaron had dispatched the demons that were available to his skill long ago, fashioned them into something he could see and kill and had killed them long ago. But now in his prime they had returned, restored by himself. By day they wandered freely everywhere. At night they were more restricted, at least in the beginning, although Aaron didn't know it had begun. Aaron was far too innocent for Emma, and the basest of the beasts she gathered around her were far too innocent too. They became her companions, her darlings. Weasel, leopard, hawk, bobcat. Coon, bat, bear, fawn, terrapin . . . Accepting meat from her lips and her love for them.

Their living shapes were so alien to Aaron. He had thought of them once only in terms of pelts and heads, of liver and spleen, of hearts, glands, and tongues roasting over burning wood in a pine branch camp. But now they seemed more alive than himself. The air quivered with the warmth of their bodies. They had made it their home here.

He wouldn't allow them in the house. He put all of his strength into keeping them out of the rooms he had made. Each night he went through the rooms one by one to make sure that none had gotten in. The windows had been nailed shut for years. On one door there were seven locks. When he was satisfied that only he and Emma were inside, he prepared dinner for them. The two of them sat eating their simple meals from silver plates, on a table that Aaron had designed and built for twenty. He had a gift for collecting things although he had no taste and Emma couldn't have cared less what she ate or saw or wore on her back. They ate, Aaron chewing and drinking and serving himself, and Emma sitting silently, one with the animals in her head.

After dinner, they went to bed, and Aaron lay upon Emma, his long body straddling hers, his fingers around the cold brass of the headboard, the bony hollow of his cheek pressed against the coarse hair. Outside the animals rubbed against the sides of the house, their heavy flanks slumped against the foundation stone, their lives preserved in their dark shapes as though in amber, their reality outside pressing on Aaron's sense of his own within that he feared they might fall through upon him, through his chest and into his heart.

And yet he managed to keep them out until the first child was born, keeping the sense of his own reality separate from his knowledge of theirs. In the days he'd watch them wandering freely, through the other buildings, all over his land. He'd watch them from behind the nailed windows. They didn't seem to pay slightest attention to him except when he was with Emma, but he knew that they were conscious of him, that they *knew* him. Sometimes he felt he wanted to crawl through the hole in the center of the great brass headboard, crawl through and come out somewhere else with a different shape and a soul they couldn't recognize. But then the first child was born and he knew there wasn't any use anymore in keeping them out, that there was no distinction there to them, that they were in a timeless state of permanence in a world that had transformed itself around him.

Stark had been long awaited. A cluster of cells long in the gathering. Two thousand years perhaps in the gathering. And then born. Brought up from magic, whether it be imagined or real, into memory. The proof of the powers of love and loneliness, and whether dream or solid flesh, it was, nevertheless, a child. Emma's child. Made from Emma's magic and Aaron's sin.

For after the first, Aaron truly believed himself to be a sinful man. He invented the Devil for them then. Emma didn't care. She had always been below good and evil. Her magic had never been anything trivial. No burying of teeth and hair. No communions of blood and excretions. If Aaron chose to believe in something as trivial as the Devil, Emma allowed him his foolishness.

Aaron made a chapel of his slaughterhouse, the building that had been his first stronghold here, his first shelter against the elements. He fashioned an altar, put up a picture of Christ in a silver frame, brought back a handsome brass cross from Boston. He was a frightened man. He prayed. He prayed for love and understanding.

But understanding was not there. They were there. His and Emma's children. After twelve years of waiting, there were twelve years of children. One each year. A miracle.

After the twelfth, it was said that Aaron died, of nothing, in bed.

The children knew, of course, that he had died of something.

That death is like a bee, buzzing around the mouth of the person it wants, trying to get inside. And it got inside Aaron.

But before that, in the years before the twelfth, when Aaron thought he still had time to atone, he grew fanatical. Fasted. Mutilated himself. Wandered naked through the seasons, slept in snow and thorns. In the winter of his sixth child, he had lost a toe and the tips of his ears to the cold. That spring, the buds of flowers opened darkly showing the faces of saints. And Aaron began losing his teeth, his teeth which had always been so strong before, falling into his hands, all carved indecisively by rot, dismal death's-heads in the image of himself.

Aaron abandoned God after the seventh was born. His prayers to him had been useless, making Aaron think that perhaps He did not want prayers, had never wanted prayers, but meat. Flesh and blood.

It was Emma that seemed to have the excellent relationship with God. They were like two bears in the same den.

Dismissing faith, Aaron took up with superstition. He started whittling, a dreamer's art, thinking he could save himself by making shadows of his terrors, those terrors which now had become as intimate to him as the shapes of Emma's children. His intent was to take their souls and make them into shadows, playthings. He had known the animals so well once by killing them, flaying them, stretching and skinning them, coring their brains, that now he was able to re-create them in wood with a knife that once had accomplished human sacrifice. He spent months carving each one, trying to capture every instinct, every aspiration in each line ... It calmed him, healed him a little. He thought he felt his will returning.

One night a year after the twelfth child, Aaron entered the house. The rooms were dark. Everything slept in the protection of their bodies. He walked through the rooms he had made, soundlessly, as he had once slipped through the wildness. It did not seem an unusual place. It was as he had built it. His family prospered here.

Aaron had now stopped trying to understand. He had made himself sink far below understanding with its poor distinction between the world of sorcery and men, between sickness and health.

He went into the room where once he'd slept with Emma. The smallest child lay beside the large brass bed, inside its sleeping box. Aaron stepped quietly, carefully not to wake his wife, and picked the baby up. Its dewlap swung gently, faintly yellow in the moonlight; its large blunt face was sleeping. He took the knife from his pocket, the one he whittled with, the ancient tool brought back from Guatemalan jungles. On the baby's chest was a faint crescent. Like the horned moon. Like a heel mark in the dust. He turned the baby on its stomach and ran the knife lightly down its spine, through the hair, not cutting but feeling the spine hard and iridescent beneath the blade. He raised the knife and in that instant Emma was upon him, tearing the knife from his hands, biting his face, screaming. It was a cry so terrible that Aaron knew that it had summoned all that he feared most. The baby screamed, and Emma. And into the room rushed the children ...

* * *

"Aauuuu," shrieked Angie.

Pearl's head jerked. "What is it?" she cried. "What's wrong!"

In the pool Jesse was bawling too. Big tears rolled down his shiny face.

"Tracker told me something terrible," he screamed. He hung to the tiled lip of the pool with his chubby hands. "It's not true either, it's not!"

Angie sat in the grass and shrieked. There was an awful smell. Franny had wound some flowers through Angie's curls. Pearl stumbled to her feet, dizzy, her head pounding.

"What's happened?" cried Pearl.

"The baby needs her diaper changed, but I don't want to do it," Franny said.

"Oh yes," Pearl said, rubbing her temples. "What a commotion, yes, that's all. I must have been dozing."

"Pearl," Jesse yelled. "It's not true what Tracker said about the whales, is it!"

"Why is she wearing a diaper anyway?" Pearl asked. "Wouldn't it be better for her to go without?" She looked at Jesse dazedly. His lower lip was thrust out. His eyes were like bowls. He held to the edge and swung his body to and fro in the water. Pearl blinked.

"He said that they kill them to make lipstick. He said that they kill them sometimes just to see how much their brains weigh."

Pearl looked at him sadly. Those wonderful songs that whales sing, she thought. The way they try and protect one another.

"It's true," Tracker said.

"Don't be mean," Jane said. "You're always trying to say mean things."

"They're going to be extinct," Tracker insisted. "You only see them when they're dead."

. . . and so spiritual, Pearl thought. With all that water around them, they must get into the meditative state quite easily.

In the sea, even here, in the sea which was around her, Pearl, and the children, there would be whales still, traveling and calling, calling one another across thousands of miles and galloping toward one another through the impossible depths of the sea, through the faint and changing lights of the sea, singing and calling and faithful to one another ...

Oh to be a diver in deep seas, to know creatures like them, to have the experiences of things! That was the secret of a woman's unfathomable smile, was it not? That she had been a diver in deep seas and been dead many times, that she had lived in a manner both sinister and undisclosed, a perpetual life of ten thousand experiences?

Pearl stroked a child's head.

One of the children said, "Whale calves in their first six months gain several hundred pounds a day."

Like a nightmare, really, Pearl thought, the growing ...

She looked from one child to another. Sam was not there. He had slipped away from them again and gone up to the house to be with her, the old woman, his grandmother. Pearl looked into the children's faces. Who could open the door of a child's face? It was like a door opening upon the growing ...

What had Sam said when she asked him if he loved her, Pearl? Yes, he had said. Yes.

But it wasn't true. It was the old woman that he loved.

CHAPTER TEN

Pearl had never found Sam's grandmother to be very lovable, but of course she saw her differently than Sam. The old woman did not like Pearl and Pearl couldn't blame her for that, and they had never spoken to one another in seven years and Pearl was actually relieved about that, but Pearl did wish that she was not quite so eccentric in her appearance.

Sometimes Pearl, in viewing the two of them together through the open door, wanted to rush through and take the child out of there, away from her speech, away from her face, which seemed terrible to Pearl. But she didn't feel she had the right. The fact of it was that the old woman was raising Sam and Pearl was not. The old woman took better care of Sam than Pearl did and always had. She had taught him how to tell a story and how to listen to one. She told him wonderful things. What advice could Pearl give if she ever had him to herself? When one is drunk and trying to eat at the same time it is helpful to make the attempt before a mirror? It was hopeless. There were tall roses in the garden that Pearl suspected of disliking her. Once she was positive that a curtain blowing in the window had been sent to murder her. It was too depressing, her flickering world. What could she say to the child? What hope could she give him? Sometimes she would wake in the night to see fifty birds, dead, but rigid in the attitudes of life, scattered on the blanket of her bed. With a groan, they would rise and be gone. She sweated. She shook. Her eyes filmed with things galloping, burrowing, flying, nesting there. And love seemed to be a kingdom from which she had been banished. The appearances of things were like scabs upon her soul, a crust which kept her soul from light. How could she tell Sam this? He was her fear.

He was her fear because of his love for the old woman. The way she appeared to Pearl was terrible. The way she appeared to Sam was not. How could they discuss it? To Pearl, she was a presence so primal, belonging to a world so little realized, that it seemed preferable to ignore her. The others did. They had, as far as she could tell, forgotten she existed. They believed in Emma more. Sam took care of his grandmother's needs and she demanded nothing of the others. She lived half like an animal in her room, but then again, half not, rather a dignified and rapacious matriarch with a face shaped by age and conviction into the edge of an opposing weapon. Sometimes she would smile at Pearl from inside that face, and Pearl would smile helplessly back with the sickening feeling that she was collaborating with God.

Not the God of her mother's faulty and romantic vision, but the true one. A god of barbaric and unholy appearance, with a mind uncomplimentary to human consciousness.

At such times, Pearl would vow to drink either more or less. She would go to her room and brush her teeth. She would go into the library and play Clue with Trip and Peter.

"Miss Scarlet did it in the ballroom with a rope," she would say dismally, moving the tiny, real rope across the playing board with her large, nail-gnawed finger.

She would cut the syrup out of Jane's hair. She would try to eat some bread. She would take a walk down by the water. She would see Sam and kiss him. She would place her hand over his, over the birthmark that was growing on his hand. It had begun as a crescent but now it seemed more like two circles gradually approaching, about to intersect, one about to eclipse the other, with darkness where they passed.

When he'd been a baby she had tried to scrub it off.

When he'd been a baby she hadn't known what to do with him. He's been so rough and silent, so helpless in her world. And yet his eyes were so fierce and wonderful. His tiny body, so strong. She felt both reverence and disgust in watching him. She had been glad for the grandmother's presence then. It hadn't seemed inappropriate to be grateful. The old woman would come down to her room and help her take care of Sam. She would push back his hair and speak into his face. She would tell him stories.

Pearl didn't know any stories. All she'd ever heard were others' stories, every day and every night her whole life long.

Once upon a time the world came to an end in a wall of boards . . .

Once upon a time the only way to keep from falling into the sky was to cling to the roots of trees . . .

Once upon a time there was a child who wanted to run away but he had a grandmother who would not let him go.

"I am determined," the child said.

"If you run away, I will follow you," the grandmother said, "for you are my little grandchild."

"I will turn into a bird and I will fly away," said the child.

"If you turn into a bird you will need rest from flying and I will become the tree that you rest in," said the grandmother.

"If you become a tree, I will become a leaf and fall away from you," said the child.

"If you become a leaf and fall, I will become the ground that catches you," said the grandmother.

"If you become the ground, I will turn into nothing," said the child, "and you will not be able to find me."

"If you turn into nothing," the grandmother said, "then I will turn into next to nothing and be next to you."

* * *

Once . . .

Pearl had had a dream in which a man was fucking her and he went right through her and penetrated the rock behind, bringing it to orgasm. Once . . .

Pearl had gone to school as a little girl. Waiting outside the school each day was an old man who could fart unlimitedly and with great range. He could imitate the sounds of all kinds of animals. The children loved him . . .

Once . . . Pearl had traveled to Florida with her mother and father in the days when they were all alive. They had been driving in the outskirts of Tampa when they saw a man flying through the air. He flew from a little garden on one side of the road to an empty field on the other. Pearl's father almost lost control of the car. They were all very upset. They learned that the flying man was a member of the Zacchini family, a circus family who invented the human cannon ball. The outskirts of Tampa was where the Zacchini family lived. They were practicing. Pearl's father had complained to the mayor. Pearl had gotten sick that night from eating trout in a hotel.

The meaningless hazards of life. The world that slumbered beneath the world of appearances that was the same world, both painful and boring at once, savage and playful, radiant and hideous, benignant and inspired.

As a child, Pearl had fancied that there was a night animal at the foot of her bed. There was a small white light in the shape of a dancer which illuminated it. Pearl never had the feeling that the night animal was guarding her, or, on the other hand, that it was dangerous to her. It was merely there, dark and skeptical somehow of her, Pearl, the child in the bed. When she grew older and no longer saw it, she knew it was there still, skeptical and unknowable still, watching her from its invisibility, like a spider from a crack.

The unknown takes on the likeness of God. The unknown takes

on the likeness that will give it strength.

In Pearl's mind the old woman was the strongest, most dreadful thing in the world.

When Sam saw her, however, he saw his grandmother, whom he loved.

The world is made each day and each night anew, the old woman might have told Sam. Sometimes much the same, sometimes very different. One dreams and then one wakes and the dream is different. Everything is brought into being with a changing nature. Nothing lasts long under the same appearance.

Sam loved her and she must have appeared to him as a figure complementary to that love. Perhaps she was a shape in a softly faded cotton dress matted with soap beneath the arms, offering chocolate, knives and picture books with warm and spotted hands. Her joints sadly swelled, her hair neatly brushed, her skin exhaling the odors of water left in the bottom of flowered vases ...

Or perhaps she seemed more like an outlaw to him, living here in secret, amid forgotten furniture and light that had been spent a hundred years before, living in a room of bones and fur and feathers, of books chewed by mice and paintings stained with flying ants, showing him (in the sink she had made into a riverbed) how to catch fish with his hands, showing him how to climb the tree that grew outside the window (the tree beneath which Emma had buried the child that died) to the very top so that he could see through the branches (brown and dead within, but living without) the coyote who lived there waiting for the bone he'd found (after the destruction of the world) to change into a woman.

There is another spirit in everything, she told Sam. The eyes of everything are two, a pair. And one is mortal and the other immortal. The vision in one eye lives on always. The spirit is there. And the spirit can wander and occupy any form it pleases ...

Perhaps he saw her mostly as this, the vision of one eye, a being only in disguise, and he conversed with her as it is said animals converse with death, knowing, the way men can't, that death is too big to be buried in the ground, that it prefers to walk and feed among us.

Pearl had always suspected that the entire universe was made by something more than human for something less than human anyway.

From outside the old woman's room, she would overhear the way they spoke with one another, in the voices they would use. Sam never spoke that way with Pearl. With her he was cautious, almost phlegmatic. He hadn't the others' artless ways. When he played with the others, when she saw him run and climb and swim with them, he seemed like them, indistinguishable from them, but when he was alone, when she saw him standing silently, the grace of his posture seemed another grace, his shape at rest seemed to fit him poorly. That was why Pearl did not like to see him sleeping. It was as though, in sleeping, he had forgotten how to be a child.

Pearl would linger outside the room when she knew that Sam was there. The room held furniture that was not wanted anywhere else. There were murky paintings and broken chairs. The legs of a walnut dresser were placed in little dishes of poison for the ants. The metal blades of a fan stirred the air. The red eye of a hot plate glowed beneath a pan of water. The old woman rested against the window, which was curtainless and streaked with salt, and Sam sat just inside the threshold. And Pearl stood sweating without, ashamed and hopeful, entering the rhythms of their speech as a swimmer enters the sea.

Once there was a woman, the grandmother told Sam, who went into the wilderness with nothing but a dog just about to whelp. The woman built a cabin in the wilderness and soon the dog had her pups. Each day the woman would tie them up while she went out to look for food. Several times, coming back to the cabin, she would hear the voices and cries of children, but inside she would only see the pups, tied up as usual. One day, instead of leaving the house, she hid inside it and when, in a short time, she again heard the voices, she rushed into the room where the pups were tied and she saw some beautiful children laughing and playing with their dog skins lying by their sides. The woman threw the dog skins in the fire and kept the children . . .

Sam turned. He held a piece of wood in his hand.

Pearl changed from white to black for winter. There were lilacs on the dressing table. Sam was two. The old woman taught him how to smile. Pearl traced Sam's name on the mirror steamy from her bath. In the house he showed no interest in his surroundings. Outside he was happier. He wore the clothes of the older children. They would dress him as they dressed themselves. Sam was three. The fall brought storms, a drowned man on the beach. There was no head but on the arm there was a tattoo of Felix the Cat. Sam was four. His grandmother taught him all things invisible, how to think and speak and hide. Pearl took him to a rodeo in Morgansport. They watched cowboys riding in a ring. There was bronco busting, bull throwing. Pearl had gin in lemonade. Sam slipped beneath the bleachers and fell into the pen where they kept the unbroken horses. Everyone screamed but the horses' yellow hoofs seemed rooted around him. They lowered their wild heads toward his. One of the rescuers was bitten in the hand but Sam didn't get a scratch. Sam was five. Pearl traced his name in the moisture of her glass. Love was not there. Sam was there. He seemed so oddly selfless, like one whose time for duty had not yet come. Salt water seeped into the well. When they dug a new one they unearthed the graves of animals. Sam pointed out the white dwarfs in the sky. He could tell the sex of trees by the wood. He turned the paint that Timmy poured into his eyes to water. He changed a bird hanging strangled from a wire into a kite. Sam was six. The others played with him. He taught each of them something. The pupils of his eyes had slits. The old woman taught him how to stop his heart and start it again. Pearl heard this. She believed everything she saw. She heard cracklings in the night that was the rain. Sam was almost seven . . .

Pearl caught the old woman's attention. Pearl saw the bands of silver striping her cheek, the unrepentant eyes. The face was sharp and gray. The face was like a talon that could tear her apart. Pearl shrank back. Sam turned.

"Look," he said, "I'm making each of them a carving for our birthdays."

She looked at the wood scattered on the floor, at the unsubtle figures of the children, their faces blurred but their shapes captured. Sam held out the image of Sweet in which he had trapped the lines of her long, startled face, her fretfulness, her grace. He righted the others at his feet. All twelve were there, crudely and strangely done, finished but for the something which was missing in them all, the moment which all things possess, the absolute moment which is neither of the past nor the future, but of nothingness, evanescence, metamorphosis.

Sam smiled at her. He wore a white polo shirt. There were mosquito bites on his cheek, fading bruises upon his knees. His eyes were yellow and sparsely lashed. His eyes could bewitch her into thinking she saw a child in his grandmother's room, in a house by the sea, in summer.

"This is the first year I've made a present. Do you like them? Can you recognize them?"

Joe and Sweet. Timmy and Jane. Franny and Ashbel. Angie and Jesse. Peter and Trip and Tracker.

As babies they had played with the animals Aaron had made for Emma's children, those figures that seemed more desperate than toys. And even now, with Angie being the only baby, they played with them still, now more in an exercise than a game, holding them and slipping into the thoughts that they possessed, the shadows in which the child's thought becomes deer thought . . . bear thought . . . bird thought . . . resurrecting themselves as Aaron's animals which he himself had made to keep those thoughts at bay.

But these figures, though so much like the others, were children's shapes. And Sam had made them.

Pearl squatted to see them better. Sam was almost seven. Seven was the number of perfection, of completeness. The old woman had raised him to this age. Sam held one of the carvings up. The light caught it. It almost seemed that Pearl could see through it to a powdery image of something further on. The old woman had taught Sam how to do this. She had first taught him how to deceive himself in child's thoughts, and then how to deceive others as to his real nature ...

Pearl shook her head as though she were alone. Sam couldn't have made these carvings. He was just a little boy, too young, even, to handle knives. Pearl had gotten confused. There were just the carvings that Aaron had made. There weren't any other ones. Aaron had seen the things he carved. He had lived with them. Aaron had lived in hell. Hell was a beast, the body of a beast, inside of which were other beasts ...

Pearl had gotten confused. She wasn't even with Sam now. She felt as though she had fallen. She stood up. The door blew shut.

CHAPTER ELEVEN

"Pearl, don't go, where are you going?"

Pearl was standing by the pool. The children tugged her hand.

"Why were you on your hands and knees, Pearl? Were you going to be sick?"

Ashbel said, "Sit down, Pearl. Peter's going to do a trick."

They pushed her gently back into the chair. The pool was empty now except for a raven drinking from the step at the shallow end. The raven was the bird who failed to return when Noah sent him from the ark. It was cursed with a terrible thirst. The raven's wings shone like oil. It dipped its beak, it raised it to heaven. August was a thirsty month.

Pearl emptied the last of the wine into her glass. The label floated in the glints of ice. Cherubim on a black background.

"I have a new trick," Peter said. "Watch."

He made the others form a circle around him. He wore blue trousers upon which he had painted orange lightning bolts. The boy was utterly possessed by magic. He wanted to saw the other children in half and shoot bullets in their teeth. Thomas prevented him from doing this. Peter claimed he had an old wand of Herrmann's which had once produced fistfuls of cigars from President Ulysses S. Grant's beard. Peter did not even want to be called Peter. He wanted them to call him Ibis the Invincible, although no one ever would.

He had high flat cheekbones and long, fine hair, but, like Trip, he was always altering his features with ink, preferring Indian designs he copied from the Straight-Arrow cards that someone had once collected from the boxes of Shredded Wheat. Ultimately he wanted to be everything: mentalist, conjurer, escape artist. He spent hours working in his cluttered room where objects were known to have been lost for years.

His room was an exotic market full of baubles and surprises, a fleshly heap of Arabian Bead mysteries, Devil's handkerchiefs, Egyptian Water Boxes, Mystic Coins, Belts of Lightning, Flying Fish, Appearing Canes, Jumping Silks, Enchanted Cigarettes, Burmese Bangles and Vampire Blocks. The fact that the impossible was rooted in his own arduous labors did not diminish its enchantment for him. He was a true magician, forever amazed at the successes he had so carefully worked out. Occasionally, he would even demonstrate the workings of an illusion. Everyone knew about the inside of his Inexhaustible Cylinder. The inner walls of the cylinder seemed smooth but they were actually slightly slanted and concealed secret compartments filled with odd objects and held closed by tiny catches. Knowing this never spoiled the trick for the other children because they never knew what would be hidden there.

"Prepare to be dumbfounded!" Peter shouted, and began to drag a string of Christmas-tree lights out of his mouth.

"Oh wow!" Timmy screamed. He wished that he could drag stuff like that out of his stomach whenever he wanted to. It was so terrifically disgusting. All that stuff, pocked with stomach acids and flecked with Orange Crush and Scooter Pie.

The lights fell on their loopy wet wire to the grass. They weren't glowing. In fact they were a little grimy, like flower bulbs shaken from a bin. The lights coiled and climbed, green and red and blue, around Peter's legs, looking insinuating and alive.

He drew an elaborate star from his mouth. The star was large with sharp points. The tips were brown with rust. Peter twitched his shoulders excitedly.

"What do you think?" he addressed them hoarsely. "Is it well done? It's not true, I know you know that, but is it well done?"

Pearl applauded. The children hooted and clapped. Clouds moved fast across the sky and Peter seemed backlit, blunt around the edges in the waning afternoon. On the horizon was a boat, no bigger than a child's thumb. The first drops of rain fell with another roll of thunder.

"We must get back to the house," Pearl exclaimed. "It's dangerous being here."

"I love electrical storms," Trip said. "Do you know that a dead tree struck by lightning can come back to life?"

"Yes," said Pearl.

"Do you believe that?" Trip asked, amazed.

"Please," Pearl said, "everybody now, run up to the house."

They scattered joyfully and ran. Pearl careened after them. By the time she reached the porch, she was soaked. She stood panting for a moment. This house was her home. It seemed improbable even after all these years. But it was the only one she had unless she could consider her body her home, a disheartening thought— this shabby tower of bones and water in which she more or less permanently resided, a lonely place and yet one always occupied to say nothing of visited continuously, shared with guests and occupied by travelers, full of tumult and disturbance and greed and sharing. Some visitors lingering only briefly, others staying a long, long time; one guest being fantastic, another quite dull. Prudes and incontinents, mommies and murderers, philosophers and mice. The body the home. One could entertain almost any notion there. Poor dump.

She ducked inside. There wasn't a child to be seen. Shivering, she stepped into the kitchen. Miriam was there dribbling little vials of food coloring into bowls of frosting. She was crying. She always cried when she made cakes for the children's birthdays.

"The cakes look delicious," Pearl said.

There were five cakes cooling on racks. Pearl went over to dry herself by the oven. Miriam sighed and mopped at her face with the back of her hand.

"Johnny would have been thirteen this year," she said. "I wouldn't recognize him."

Pearl looked at the clock over Miriam's head. REGULATOR it said on the glass coffining the pendulum.

Miriam sat on a stool and slathered frosting on a cake.

"He used to wait for me to finish with my baking so I could read a story to him. He loved stories. I had an old book with big black and white pictures. *The Good Luck Story Book* it was called. And sometimes I would just make things up while I combed his hair. He had very fine, curly hair, always tangled, and I would comb it out while he sat on my lap. I would speak about each curl that I untangled as though it were the home of some living thing. I called my Johnny's head a 'curiosity shop.'

"'Here now,' I would say. 'Here now, here's a little bird's nest. But where are the birds? Have they flown away? And, oh, hear that pig squeal! That couldn't be you! And here, look at this wrapped up so carefully, I'll have to pull hard. Oh what a roar! There must be a lion in there ...'"

"I know it's terrible, Miriam, but please, Franny and Ashbel ..." Pearl stared at the stain on the butcher block. The children had spilled dye that spring when they had been coloring Easter eggs.

"The darkness has him now," Miriam said, "and the darkness is not going to give him back. Now that man from New Zealand who had sent the bit of rabbit fur from his little girl's muff, now think of him. His little girl had died from fever when she was five and he and his wife thought they'd never get over it but within the year they had another baby daughter who now is five and although she doesn't in the least resemble the lost girl, she can remember everything about her, everything, favorite toys and places and food. I think that's wonderful ... imagine the comfort she can provide ..."

Pearl looked at the clock. The hands hadn't moved. Time for a drink, she thought. Mustn't miss my appointments. It must be awful, she thought, to have a child who could remember the day it died.

On the wall was a long and silly donkey she had drawn for the children's birthday. The donkey's buttocks were crucified with long needles to which scraps of paper had been glued. And there, beneath it, orderly, arranged, were rolls of bright crepe streamers, a dozen packages of balloons, an assortment of cheap and lively favors. Motion books, buzzer rings, snapping gum packs, make-up kits, vari-vues.

She moved one of the vari-vues slowly between her fingers. A bride and groom kissing. Again and again. Another showed a child jumping rope. Over and over the feet skipped, the head flew back, the rope completed its arc.

Franny liked to jump rope. Pearl had heard her sing:

> "Fudge-Fudge call the Judge
> Mama has a newborn baby
> It's not a girl
> It's not a boy
> It's just a newborn baby."

"I know," Miriam said, "I must stop this. People depend upon me, don't they? Living people. And I depend upon them, upon the constancy of strangers, sorrows, the same sorrows, undergone over and over for nothing ..." She squeezed her lips together.

Pearl came toward her. "Poor Miriam, can I help?"

"Oh no," she said gently, surprised. Her gaze settled on Pearl as if for the first time. "You're shivering," she said. "You should get dry."

"All right," Pearl said.

"You're worse than the children," Miriam sighed. "Look how you've puddled my kitchen."

Pearl went into the library, where the bar was. The oriental rug in front of the cabinet of bottles was worn in strips.

"I'm not the only one who's ever had a drink in this house," Pearl muttered as she poured gin into a glass.

Thomas' voice startled her.

"Ahh, Pearl," he said, "your looks are positively medieval today. You have the disease of that time, languor and emaciation."

Pearl looked at Thomas' handsome, imperturbable face. She looked at the *Atlantic* that was on the coffee table.

Pearl, look! a child screamed in her head, I can eat with my feet!

The rain covered the glass with artificial night like a dark archangel and then lifted and was gone. The wan light of the interrupted day fell into the room.

Pearl ignored Thomas. Instead, she looked downward. Beside the bar was a wastebasket made from a rhinoceros' foot. It held a crushed can of grapette. The rhinoceros must have been a beautiful specimen once, although it certainly had been secured only by altering its appearance considerably. It made Pearl sad.

She walked out of the library and began her careful ascent of the stairs, careful not to falter or spill. On the wall was an alphabet made from misshapen twigs glued to a piece of plasterboard. An idea Trip had struck upon at the age of three. And there was the tile rubbing that Sweet had done. Something definitely carnal was going on there.

By the time she had reached the first landing, her gin was almost gone. She couldn't remember sipping it, but she couldn't recall feeling it slide down her leg either.

On the second landing, Pearl oriented herself by the bookcase there upon which old photographs were jumbled with rare first editions. Pictures of the island the century before. The family through the generations. Ladies and gentlemen always, in launches and on lawns. Children grinning happily over one thing or another. A barbecue behind the stone house. People looking into a pit over which some charred animal turned. A tree limb upon which ten people sat. And views, many views. And of course in the center of it all, the founding father, Aaron, and the foundered ma.

Before her children had been born, Emma cradled heaps of rabbit skins and sang to them.

Pearl never went by without glancing at Emma's picture. She fancied that she resembled her in some mocking way. Nothing literal, but something, an image in the bones. Perhaps it was just her thinness. The shadows beneath her eyes.

Isn't that the way with most of us, Pearl thought . . . going to all that trouble, living and dying for all those years we're in the process of it, only to be remembered in the end by those who never knew us, by a single photograph which might not have been accurate at all . . .

One of the children had left a partially eaten cracker on the top shelf. It had a banana or something spread on it. Pearl picked it up and put it in her mouth. Pearl liked eating the odds and ends of the children's leftovers. She would pick up half-gnawed apples, tip the warm drops of cereal milk into her mouth, chew the gristle of the bones they left behind. She liked seeing them eat, the way they ate with open, happy mouths.

Pearl climbed the last few steps and walked down the corridor to her room. On her dresser was a bottle of gin and a bottle of quinine. She poured some gin into her glass. She looked at the bottles and sighed.

She turned toward the bathroom and saw a beetle making its tortured way across the floor. It was a thing the size of her thumb with a dull, gleaming skeleton and peculiar open jaws. The wings were transparent. The eyes were on stalks protruding from the head.

There would be something for Ashbel's collection, Pearl thought fleetingly. It lurched beneath her foot. She heard the crack of its carapace.

It looked clean and swept around this house but it was not clean and swept. There were nasty, irrational things here. Lower life forms that wore away good intentions and a zest for happiness.

She went into the bathroom on tiptoe and wiped the insect off her sole. She ran water for a bath, took off her bikini and sat naked on the toilet seat, sipping her gin and watching the tub fill. She hummed a little.

She lowered herself into the tub. She shivered and burrowed down up to her neck. She took another sip of gin and then put the glass on the toilet, whose functions were concealed discreetly. A wicker chair with a hinged seat had been placed over the bowl. Someone's concept of the seemly. At the back of the bowl there was a stain on the porcelain. It resembled an angel to Pearl in her giddier moments. Or at least that part of an angel which had wings, and what more was there to an angel really? A minor bidet god. A girl angel or a boy angel down there. Difficult to tell. Like snakes. There's a mystery. How do snakes do it?

Pearl soaped her skinny face. She felt a little better. She closed her eyes. Tomorrow was the children's birthday. She should go into town and get each of them something. Certainly she should get Sam something, her own child, after all.

She felt a wave of nausea and tipped her head back. The water lapped against her ears.

Seven years old. Thomas said that at seven one possesses the emotions that one will be guided by forever. Thomas said that at seven you stopped being a child and got the face by which you would be known or not known. When Pearl had been seven, she'd laid on the sand at her parents' summer place and let the waves push her softly around. Actually what she'd been doing was pretending that she was the victim of a shipwreck, quite dead. Or nearly so. When she wasn't doing that, she was bouncing on the bed in her room, stripped to her Lollipops and sparring with herself. She had never known what she was. She hadn't the slightest clue, particularly at seven.

The water grew cold. Pearl got out. She began dressing before she realized she hadn't dried herself. She hesitated, regarding the bed, the bottles, the window beyond which the sea stretched, glittering and gray, then finished dressing and pulled on her shoes. Looking at herself in the mirror, she realized she wasn't dressed so much for dinner as for a walk. Perhaps she wouldn't eat dinner tonight. Alcohol was food. What did it matter? She would eat cake tomorrow. She hated sitting down to dinner. Hated the Géricault painting above the sideboard. Twenty horses' asses above them every night as they ate.

Pearl made her way back down to the core of the house. She heard Thomas' voice.

". . . more advanced than Soleri. He's very involved in temperature control, creating ecologies which function independent of outside energy sources. I'd like to experiment with something like that here . . . I . . ."

Pearl rolled her eyes.

The colors of the island were drained with the approach of dusk and the sea looked fat and high from the rain. It always amazed Pearl that the island was here at all. It seemed the merest accident. If the ocean were a few feet higher, and there didn't seem to be any reason it shouldn't be, most of the land would vanish. And yet the island was complete. It had rivers and ponds, deep, dead woods where the trees had been killed by vines and green sunny woods of oak and hickory. It had fruit orchards and oyster beds and fifty-foot dunes. Pearl had never explored it much really. The children told her about these things.

She took a path behind the house that curved to the beach, passing through the broken gates and the tumbled-down pens that hadn't been used since Aaron's day. She often wondered why the children didn't have pets here. They could have had ponies and goats and calves . . . But they didn't seem interested. In all the years that Pearl had been here not a single child had had as much as a kitten or a puppy.

She walked through the scrub woods, her knees buckling slightly. She almost fell. She stopped, then sat down. She was sitting there quietly, rather stupidly, she supposed, when she saw a raven drop from the branches of a tree and waddle self-importantly toward her. Perhaps it was the same raven she had seen drinking from the swimming pool. It moved toward her rapidly, its black eye dedicated to her. It pecked her leg.

Pearl waved her arms at it. It drew itself back up into the trees. It seemed genuinely amazed that Pearl was still alive.

Pearl scrambled to her feet. What a calamity her life was! She hurried along the path, her eyes fixed on her shoes moving forward. She could not remember why she had wanted to take this walk. Just simple desire for communion with the essential ultimate, she supposed.

She emerged from the woods down an incline that led through a muted tangle of bayberry and broom sedge and ruined roses. She walked in a valley behind the dunes, smiling to herself as she lurched along, her shoes filling up with sand. The champagne-colored sky met the sea serenely before her, but off to the north she could see rain falling in a ribbon of gray. Small white suns sailed before her eyes, the gin, she supposed, although it could be falling stars. August was the time for them. Perhaps her brain had become so sensitive to all those neurons exploding that she could now witness stars in the daytime, although it was hardly the day now, more the dusk, the benighted hour. And there was a star, burning itself up, drifting and gone even before it made its presence manifest to human eyes. No longer supported by whatever cared to keep it in place. Like the plane seven years ago had fallen from the sky . . .

She could hear the children calling out from their beds in other nights:

". . . Cassiopeia's Chair. And that's Aquila the Eagle and Vulpecula the Fox . . .

. . . and Lacerta the Lizard . . .

. . . and Equuleus the Colt . . ."

Out of the ribbon of gray rain falling, Pearl saw a figure running, a horse pounding up the beach. Rather it looked like a horse, although she knew it was Joe, white trousers flapping, white hair streaming, the double being of horse and rider.

Imagine him mounted, thought Pearl, imagining, a little ashamed of herself. But it was a fact any woman would tell you. There was something about a mounted man. Something about a mounted man that made a woman feel that nothing else would do.

Pearl took a few more steps and then sat down, legs crossed, head just cresting a shallow dune. She watched Joe run. He was still far away. His feet running made the water foam. Horse and water. Such a pretty thing to see. Horses *were* so stupendous in the mind. Once the children had nailed a horseshoe above the door to her room. It hadn't brought her much luck as far as she could see, but it wasn't supposed to be for luck, the children said, it was for keeping the nightmares away, although it hadn't worked in that regard either. Perhaps it had been put up upside down. Pearl hadn't noticed it for some time now. It probably wasn't there anymore.

She put her chin in her hands and listened to the strokes of the waves, the stirring of pebbles on the shore as the water was sucked in and out.

She heard a peculiar sound, a scuffling, a hissing.

"How's the fit, my dear?" a man's voice said. A woman giggled.

Pearl held her breath. Sometimes picnickers came over by boat from Morgansport. They anchored off the bay side and then came over to the ocean beach. They always made a mess. The children discouraged them the best they could.

The man's voice muttered, "Get back here with that bottom, goddamn it. Put it right up here."

"You gonna put your frightful hog in my little ass," the woman said, still giggling.

Pearl inched across the sand until she could see the pair, between two dunes and just slightly below her.

There was a small radio playing on a blanket. The man was short with curly red hair. His freckled complexion gave him a strained, intemperate look. His penis was like a rod, mushroom-gleaming. The woman was wearing only the top of her bikini. She was standing, facing the man, a little unsteady on her feet, smoking and laughing.

"C'mon, sugar," the man wheedled.

"I've got a mind of my own, you know," she said. "You just wait a minute."

"Oh, sugar, your mind's in your box, and that's just where it should be. You shouldn't worry about that one bit." In a swift movement, he turned the woman around, pressed his arms across her back and pushed himself in between her haunches. She hissed slightly. A sound like water on a skillet. The man's hand caressed her belly. He seemed to be staring sightlessly at Pearl, pushing into the woman all the while like a bull nudging against a crib. They rocked together as one. The man's lips curled back over his clenched teeth.

Pearl was terribly shocked. What if one of the children had come across this, these awful people doing this? One of the poor little children, searching the beach for shells, for baby cradles and turkey feet ...

"Jesus Christ," she heard the man cry, "what in fuck's sake is that!"

She saw Joe, rearing, falling down upon them, legs raised, powerful chest sparkling with shell. He struck the man heavily with an unshod foot. The woman squealed and went down beneath him as he rolled. Joe's place had been taken by this whinnying, blasphemous thing, all hoofs and teeth in the instant it took before the eye could see it was a boy again, laughing and cursing them.

The man reached for the radio and flung it, screeching the news. Joe ducked. He raised a callused, chestnut-colored foot, a foot so hard he could kick a rock like a football. Pearl saw the thick, deeply ridged nails. She saw him catch the man with one last, fast kick in the neck before he raced off.

The man lay belly up on the sand, one hand on his throat, the other on his wilted meat. The woman pulled up her bikini bottoms. She went over to the radio and picked it up. She jiggled it.

"Why didn't you throw something else at him?" she said, clicking the dials of her radio disconsolately on and off.

"Crazy wild fucker," the man gasped, "I'll kill him."

"Ha, ha, ha," the woman said succinctly. And then in a rush, "He about killed *you*. We're trespassing here, you know. Maybe they could shoot us, you know. First the rain and now this. Just because you're too cheap to take us to a Quality Court."

Pearl curled up in a ball. She heard the man panting and grunting and then she heard the beach grass whining against their legs as they moved through it and then she heard nothing but the stones moving in the waves again. She looked at the spot where they had been and where Joe had been. Beer cans were scattered everywhere. The sand was trampled and wet.

Pearl stood up cautiously, her shoulders hunched. She had just wanted to take a pleasant walk. She had just wanted to clear her head a bit before settling down to the evening's drinking. Darkness was moving into her head like a tide, lapping gently, enveloping her. Perhaps she would die this moment here of a massive insult to the brain, the way that poets did.

She dropped over the dune to the harder sand of the beach. She walked in the direction from which Joe had come. She could still see a trace of his running feet. About a quarter of a mile up the beach there was a wider jeep trail that circled around to the house. She would take that way back.

Once when Pearl had been a child, she had bent over to pat a dog and another dog had leapt upon her back. She could not get the vision of those disreputable fornicating intruders out of her mind.

The children could not bear intruders here. They were really quite rude to them. Well, more than rude certainly, if half of what they intimated and half of what she saw was true.

And what had she seen actually? Joe was Joe but he had been something else as well.

Pearl walked, heels and toes sucking in the sand pools in which miniscule fish hung. Mussels gleamed on the dimming rocks.

"Pearl ..." She heard her name flying from a child's throat. "Puuuuurl ..." It hung on the salty wind like a scrap of tune from a hymnal, a hymn about burdens that could not be laid down. To be human was to be homeless, furthest removed from the blessing of God. Pearl. Pearl the mad and homeless. Pearl the afraid.

"You've no need to be frightened, Pearl," the children would call through the door when they heard her having a terrible dream, "there's no one here but us."

She would lie on her stomach. She would cover her head with a pillow. The nightmare was like a thing come to kiss and lick you. When you lay on your stomach and it realized it was not kissing your face, it would get mad and go away.

"Puuuuurl ..." It was a child's voice, calling her to supper. In a few more moments it would be dark.

She picked her way through the rocks and ribbons of sea weed. The sea slapped on the rocks. The night birds flew with open mouths. The sky was full of stars that cast no light. It was becoming increasingly difficult for her to distinguish things and she was just able to make out the trail that swept out of the woods to the beach. Her mouth tasted as though she were holding metal in it. When she got back to the house, she could get another drink. She hurried toward the line of stunted trees.

"Sweet," she said, startled.

The girl was standing timidly in the shadows. Pearl felt an urgency to the night coming. It was charged with the sense of things, the hidden signals of things.

Pearl remembered the dread she'd felt at her own first menstruation, but she said:

"You mustn't feel embarrassed. It's a wonderful thing to become a woman."

Pearl was lying to herself, afraid of herself. To become a woman was to become a question when as a child one was all swift and shining answer.

"Let's go back to the house together," Pearl said. She drew closer, about to put her arm around Sweet's shoulders. She smelled it coming off her, the sad corporeal odor. The girl's face was puffed and almost ugly. Her eyes were dry and burning in her head.

As Pearl approached, those eyes widened, then became fixed, the pupils dilating so that the irises filled the sockets' orbits and sank back into her head. It seemed she wanted to run in the instant that she was still. And it was only for that instant that it seemed strange, before she was gone, before her form was gone. Her belly turned soft and swinging beneath her, holding her up. Her arms began to turn as long and tapered as her legs. Her face swung out flat and her nose turned black and became part of a soft, dark muzzle. And when that instant passed, and it seemed she wanted to speak, her tongue had then become a thick deer's tongue and the hand she raised was a deer's hoof, black and graceful, and her flanks were covered with tight, bright fur.

Pearl screamed. The deer bounded into the trees and vanished.

Sam was shining a light on her.

"Nooooo," Pearl screamed.

"What is it Pearl?" His voice sounded frightened. She was heartened for a moment by that tone of fear, but then she realized she must make him know that she would not be deceived by him.

"Stop it!" she screamed.

He fumbled for the switch on the battery-powered lamp and turned it off.

"It's me, Sam," he said quickly. "I just came to get you for supper."

It was not Sam. It was that child that had never been Sam. She felt him in the darkness before her with a sickening sense of foreboding, like an amputee might feel a missing limb.

"Did the deer scare you?" He came closer. "I saw it too."

"It wasn't a deer," she said.

. . . and it wasn't a horse she'd seen when she saw Joe . . .

"You've come to do this, haven't you?" she said.

He was a changeling, the old woman's child. He had used this place to grow in, to learn how to seem a child, but he would be leaving this place soon. He could not stay here forever. He would leave with the one who had taught him to do these things. And after he left, he would still want the children here to be a part of him. He wouldn't want to leave them without leaving behind in them something which understood him.

"It's all right, Pearl. Come up to the house. You need something to eat and then you can go to bed."

He turned the lamp back on. It glowed beneath his unrecognizable face.

"Why are you doing this?" Pearl asked.

But she knew. Humans were changed into animals because of some sorrow, some punishment, or some mercy shown by the gods.

"Have you been sent here to save me?" she said, her voice trembling.

"Please, Pearl," he said. "Everything is all right."

He took her hand. She let him.

CHAPTER TWELVE

As a child, Pearl's mother told her, "You must never look at the sun. Never, never, look at the sun . . ."

As a child, idly dialing her own number, she discovered that it spelled out FOREVER.

She wished that she could dial FOREVER on the telephone and hear it ring. It would ring and ring. She would probably give up just as the receiver was being lifted on the other end.

There was a smell of perfume in the room. Pearl smelled wonderful. Someone must have spilled a bottle all over her.

She opened her eyes. She was in bed, naked beneath the sheets. Franny stood by Pearl's dressing table, making up her eyes with Pearl's mascara. Her arms were shiny with perfume and her eyes were a painted black mask. A horizontal figure 8. The sign of life as an empty cord.

"What have you done with your face?" Pearl said.

The sun began to take the room apart, appropriating things one by one and exposing them to Pearl's eyes.

"Pearl's awake," Franny cried delightedly. "Pearl's awake!" She rushed to the bed and kissed her arm.

Some of the other children ran into the room.

"Pearl, I had this wonderful dream," Ashbel shouted. "I had a dream about a horse that when I got on him he became a part of me and flew through the air faster than a plane. He had a little knob on his saddle like a little wheel and I could make him go anywhere."

Franny looked at him disgustedly. "That's Scheherazade. That's from *The Arabian Nights*. You can't say Scheherazade as though you're saying your own."

"Here, Pearl, I made you some tea." Jane held out a child's play teacup.

"No," Pearl said. "Please." She rubbed her face. Her cheeks ached. Her mouth felt like a bit of fruit wobbling in setting Jello.

Jane thrust out her lower lip. "I've been waiting hours for you to wake up," she said. "I've been waiting and waiting and waiting."

Pearl took the cup and quickly tasted its rim.

"She drank it," Timmy whispered in his little furry voice, full of dreams and hurts.

Pearl dropped the cup. It spilled on the sheet, making a lavender stain. "What was it?" Pearl cried.

"Just water," Jane said. "With a crayon crunched up in it. Really, Pearl, that's all."

Pearl looked for the clock on her night table, tipped against the bottle of gin. She righted it. Half-past six. She groaned.

Tracker was standing by the bed eating bread and jelly. He made a snapping, smacking sound. Pearl struggled back against the pillows, drawing the sheets up to her chin.

"Where is Sam?" Pearl said.

"He's right here, Pearl."

"Did I say something terrible to you last night?" she asked. "I have a feeling I said something very terrible."

"No," he said. "You didn't."

"What was I doing?" she muttered. "What was I thinking?"

"Do you want some aspirin?" Ashbel asked.

"Yes." To Franny she said, "Please wash that stuff off your face." She had a terrible headache. Once Miriam had told her that she knew the moment when half her life was over.

"Death," Miriam had said, "was born in me the seventeenth

of March 1947."

She said it felt like a headache.

"I'm going to die," Pearl cried. "I've misunderstood it all. I've gotten it all wrong and still everything is going to be over with, everything is going to be gone."

"You're not going to die," Timmy said. "We'll take care of you." He hugged her. He was wearing a pair of overalls that were very soft, almost like velvet. She petted his shoulder. Some memory stirred. She looked at his grave, sleek little face.

All the other children were naked to the waist. They all had funny-looking marks on their chests.

"What is that?" she demanded. "What have you done to yourselves now? Oh I'm so tired, I can't bear this anymore. I can't think." And it was true. Her mind was like the troubled, whiskey-colored sea. "Please be nice to one another," she begged.

"Wake up, Pearl, wake up," Jane sang.

Jesse said, "It's a sign we made for ourselves, Pearl. We're a secret."

"*We're* not a secret," Trip said. "Our *society* is secret."

Pearl drew Jane closer to her and squinted at the red mark between her pale nipples.

"It looks as though someone stepped on you," Pearl said.

"Oh no, we drew it." She puffed out her stomach proudly.

"Was it Sam's idea?" Pearl asked suspiciously.

"Yes, Pearl, it was Sam's idea," the children yelled.

"Sam," Pearl persisted. She plucked at the sheet. She stared at him. He held out his hand and patted her fist on the sheet. She grasped it, traced the birthmark on his hand with her fingers.

"Sam doesn't have a mark on *his* chest," Pearl said.

The children hesitated at this. Jane squeezed up her little pansy face.

Ashbel said, "Shall I put the aspirin in your mouth, Pearl?"

Pearl did not want to let go of Sam's hand. She looked at the dark, almond-shaped center of the two rough circles on his hand. It was so pronounced now. She had never seen it so clearly before.

"Sam's your leader so he doesn't have to have that mark, is that right?" Pearl asked. "But it's ink, isn't it? And you could hurt yourselves, you know. You could get blood poisoning. Didn't Trip get blood poisoning once? I wish you wouldn't draw on yourselves so much."

"I never got blood poisoning, Pearl. Once I broke my finger in an oarlock is all." Trip was using Pearl's comb on his hair.

Ashbel was pushing the aspirin dutifully in Pearl's mouth.

"No, no," she protested. She tossed her head. "Owwwww," she said. I need a drink, she thought. Hair of the dog that bit.

"Peter," she said, "what are you doing by my bottles, come away . . ."

Peter jumped around, hands waggling by his face.

"Everything is dim," he shrieked. "Everything is blackness!" The two bottle caps he had put over his eyes glinted whitely.

"Peter looks like Orphan Ornie," Jane said seriously around her thumb.

Pearl managed a smile. She still held Sam's hand.

"Did you even draw on poor Angie?" she asked sadly. "Poor little . . ."

The baby was crawling over the sheets, nibbling at its printed leaves. Pearl looked at her sorrowfully. "I will tell you one of the great secrets of life, Angie," she said. "One of the great secrets of life is learning to live without being happy." She stirred restlessly, impatient with herself. "Get out of here, now, all of you, I must get dressed. I must look awful. Franny, get me my mirror so I can see how awful I look."

"I used it for my town, Pearl. I had to. It's the lake in my town."

"It's just as well," Pearl said. The thought rather enchanted her. No more mirrors. No more the witnessing of struggles between time and her selves.

Franny kissed her. "Thank you, Pearl."

Tracker had finished eating. His hair was brindle in the early morning light. His nails were long and dirty.

Jesse said, "Franny's lake is frozen. People can't swim in it. Pearl," he asked, "what do you call a man deer?"

"Pearl, remember when you found a bottle in the water with a message in it?" Tracker said.

"Yes," Pearl said. It had said "Hello." It hadn't even wished her luck. Pearl's mouth was sour and dry. Her stomach trembled. One drink right now would enable her to think better, she knew it would. One drink would make her feel better. But she had to stop drinking. She was a wicked woman, a terribly wicked woman and a drunk. She would stop drinking entirely. Perhaps a beer now and then. No, not even that. Nothing. Her mind lurched forward and she could feel Sam trying to slip his hand away.

What had happened last night? What had been said? Perhaps nothing had been said. Words are inadequate for anything other than human concerns. But what then had been thought? That was the important thing. She thought of the bottle floating. All the bottles emptied, gone. *Goodbye.*

Ashbel was saying something to her. It didn't seem to be his words he was using. She couldn't understand him. It was his teeth. They were so big and wide, really malformed.

"Pearl," Timmy said, "I dreamed last night a black dog was chasing me. I was awful scared."

"That's a Devil dream," Trip said. "You know Judas was possessed by the Devil and when the devil was cast out of him by Jesus, the Devil ran off in the shape of a black dog."

"It didn't do Jesus much good to get rid of the Devil in Judas," Peter said. He was making a rapid jerking motion with his head.

"Don't do that," Pearl said.

"Well Trip thinks he knows things but he doesn't."

"Don't quarrel in here," Pearl begged, "I have such a headache. Now, get out of here, all of you, please." She dropped Sam's hand. Angie crawled across her stomach. Her lame leg felt heavy and flat. "I have to think," Pearl said, "I have to get up."

"It's our birthday day today, Pearl, you didn't forget did you?" Timmy said.

Pearl's heart pounded. She remembered writing something down. She remembered bending down to pat a dog and another dog leaping upon her back. The physicality of beasts. Their preposterous ways! Or had that been in a dream? She remembered now. She had had an amazing dream last night and she had written it down.

"Are you coming for breakfast, Pearl? Miriam's making waffles. She's making round ones."

"Yes," Pearl said, her stomach sickening at the thought. "Yes, yes, go away now."

Pearl slowly got out of bed. On the bureau there were red hairs in her comb. By her glass and bottles there was a feather which Peter had left behind.

On the other side of the door, she could hear Tracker's voice saying, "Mad people smell like the sea. You can tell. The smell comes right off them."

Did she smell like the sea? Pearl went into the bathroom, where she filled the sink with cold water. She took a deep breath and pushed her face into the water. Movie stars did this, didn't they? For their complexions? They used snorkels.

It didn't make her feel any better. She mopped her head dry. She dressed moodily, looking at the empty spot on the wall where the mirror had hung. Moodily she went into the bedroom and looked out at the quilted hot sky. She heard one of the children singing:

"Once there were three fishermen
Once there were three fishermen
Fisher, Fisher
Men, Men, Men
Fisher, Fisher
Men, Men, Men
Once there were three fishermen."

She looked about the room for something she might have written upon the night before. There didn't seem to be anything. She sat on the bed and looked at the screen in front of the fireplace. Hammered into the brass of the screen were hunters shooting birds out of trees. She screen shone unevenly. The hunters' mouths and eyes were clogged with whitened wax. Aaron, the hunter, had liked the motif. But in the end it was he who had been the hunted. God was the final hunter, lovingly hunting.

Pearl peered over the screen. A child's lined writing pad lay in the ashes. She pushed back the screen and picked it up. She had written upon it in crayon. The letters were crude and wavering.

I PEARL BELIEVE THAT MY SON SAMUEL

Pearl paused. Perhaps she should straighten herself out with just one drink before reading further. Her hand shook. It had been an enlightened civilization centuries ago, had it not, which instead of punishing witches punished those who believed in witches? She had never been punished. She had never been punished enough.

IS NOT A HUMAN CHILD HE WITH THE OLD WOMAN
WHOSE HE IS

Pearl's hand felt numb. In a way she still felt drunk, with her heart beating muddily, everything turning and falling. She looked at the words, rising.

INTO ANIMALS CHILDS DO NOT FEEL THIS HAPPENING
BUT I SEE

It was so muggy in the room. The sky was milky and sullen. Seven, the clock said. Noah had brought the animals into the ark by sevens. A clock downstairs rang six times but that was the old ship's clock. Pearl dropped the paper with more distaste than horror. The nauseous intrigues of the drunk! The suspicions and complaints! It was absolute gibberish. The wild ugly words trailed off into a thick straight crayoned line. Like a heart stopping on a cardiogram. Or a mind. The death of the mind.

Perhaps she had at last gone too far. Her brain had become shrunken and inflamed. She was hallucinatory and hateful and mean-spirited. She had always been suspicious of her Sam (and his name had never been Samuel, not ever, it just showed how drunk she'd been to write that), she had never been a decent mother to him, her only child, her only tie to life, really. He had always been sad and quiet and unknown to her but that was her fault alone. And he had always seemed different from the others, but why indeed shouldn't he be? Some deep part of him was probably still cold with the shock of that terrible plane crash. Even an infant has to be affected by a moment of horror, a moment when all around in a stinking swamp people were metamorphosing into so much meat and probate.

TO BE CLOSER TO GOD TO BE ANIMALS

What a dangerous woman she was! She crumpled the paper disgustedly and then tore it into pieces. She went back to the bed and lay upon it with a sigh. She lay with her eyes open for when she closed them she felt sick. She hated the night, the nightly battle with terror and time, but she survived it once more. This time just barely, she thought. And now it was day, a new day, a birth day. Sam was the gentlest, the most modest of all the children. To cloak him in her sickness, to make him the instrument of her disease . . . She groaned. No wonder the child had found refuge in his grandmother. Any fantasy would be preferable to Pearl's own.

She remembered once seeing the old woman on the beach. It had been the only time on the island she had seen her without Sam and she had been worried at first at seeing her there, sitting on the beach, on the shore among the stones with the sun going in and out of the clouds, making her first light and then dark. The old woman had seemed a thing eternal, come to life, a being who knew all things, the source of all Pearl lived with.

"Pearl," a child cried from the hall, "come for waffles, you must, Uncle Thomas said so."

Pearl padded out, her bare foot striking a half-eaten peach one of them had left by the door.

They were eating out on the patio. The women wanted to enjoy the last of the fading colors of the summer garden. Two large glass and wrought-iron tables were set with jugs of milk and syrup and bowls of fruit. Jesse was watering the flower beds that lay behind the brick border that Les had laid years before. He would water the flowers for a while and then just run the hose on the bricks. Then he would flip the hose up into the oak overhead, casting out birds. Then he would sprinkle it on his toes.

"Don't waste that water," Miriam called, "the well will run dry. That storm didn't soak."

"I am reading *Hamlet*, Uncle Thomas. I am enjoying it, I think," Peter said.

Thomas stood with a bright orange beach towel around his neck. He had just come up from the beach. He flipped his long hair back with his hands. Pearl felt droplets of water fall upon her arm.

"Do you know why it was that Hamlet chose not to commit

suicide?" Thomas asked.

"So he wouldn't fall into the cocoa," Ashbel giggled.

"Dope," Franny said.

Peter shook his head.

Thomas said, "Because Hamlet realized that suicides go to their death in triumph."

Ashbel giggled again. "Why did the elephant stand on the marshmallow?"

"Dope," Franny said. "You think every riddle has the same answer. Besides that, you tell jokes backwards."

Tracker was pretending to fence with a garden rake.

"How now! A rat? Dead for a ducat, dead!"

Lincoln looked at him with loathing. Tracker caught his glance and blushed. He went over to harass his brother Timmy. "Look, Tim," he said, "I'm gonna take off your thumb." He folded the little boy's hand and appeared to pluck off his left thumb between his thumb and forefinger of his own right hand.

Timmy squeaked.

Lincoln muttered something unpleasant.

"Oh please, don't do that," Pearl said to him. She hated the way Lincoln talked about his children.

He looked at her indulgently. "Children have no awareness of being disliked, Pearl. They can't relate another person's hatred of them to themselves as they have no idea what their selves are." He yawned. His belly strained against his tennis jersey.

Miriam hovered over the blackened waffle iron. A fragrant stack of waffles was accumulating beneath a nickel-plated warmer.

"Franny," she said, "pick some flowers for Mommy, will you, and put them on the table." She sighed and wiped her hands on her apron. "August is the saddest month," she said. "Everything is fading."

'Thy young glories
Leaf and bud and flower
Change cometh over them
With every hour.'"

Her voice was gentle and quavering. She plopped more batter on the grid.

"Transmutation is nature's law," Thomas said. To Pearl, he smiled. "How are you feeling this morning?"

"Oh, I'm fine, just fine," she said, smiling. "Where are Joe and Sweet?" she asked, smiling and smiling.

"They overslept, I suppose," Thomas said.

"I wish I was pretty," Franny lamented, yanking at the flowers in a careless way.

"It is not for human beings to be pretty, Franny," Thomas said. "We have language and intelligence, which has to be enough. We must leave the pretties to the animals."

Timmy pounced at a lizard near Lincoln's foot, jarring the table.

"In one of the Greek accounts of creation," Thomas went on, "the god Epimetheus was given the responsibility for distributing the ingredients of biological creation among all the creatures. He lavished everything upon the wild animals, beautiful fur and feathers, gracefulness of form, strength and agility. By the time he came to man, he had run out of desirable characteristics. Man was left with just weakness and ugliness. It was his brother Prometheus who gave man dominance to keep him from shame."

"I don't mind being ugly," Tracker said, "but I won't be weak."

Lincoln looked at him in surprise. "Oh, oh, oh," he said. "We'd better watch out now." He looked at Timmy. "What are you *doing* down there?" He nudged him with his foot.

Pearl, with trembling hand, put on a pair of sunglasses. Ev-

erything looked yellow. She took them off again. Hell was a place
of learning, a place where trees give shade, dew falls and grass
grows . . . She casually gripped her knees. The children ran about
the patio, beautiful and happy. She felt like a lump amid them, an
outrage. And the other adults even worse. Yahoos kept by wild
horses . . .

"It's going to be a hot one," Shelly said. She was pregnant
again. She wore a necklace from which dangled a gold arrow
pointing downward and the letters BABY. She hadn't gained much
weight. She was still very early on. She poured cream upon her
strawberries.

"Look here, Jane," Thomas said, "without calling this a pitcher
tell me what it is." Thomas was always doing this sort of thing
with the smaller children. Jane stared soberly at the pitcher. Timmy,
scrambling up, knocked his head against the side of the table and
knocked the pitcher over.

"Goddamn it!" Lincoln shouted.

Thomas laughed. "That's very good, Tim. Tim has it. When
there are no names, the world is not classified in limits and
bounds."

Timmy's jaws expanded sideways. He smiled. He lapped the
cream from his arm.

"Pearl, have some coffee! You're shaking."

She looked at Thomas worriedly, then absent-mindedly cut into
her waffle, which was almost afloat with syrup. She put her fork
down. In the oak tree she saw Peter's large, pale shape.

"Pearl, Pearl," Thomas admonished her. He spoke her name
stolidly, like a woodsman axing a tree.

Sam sat some distance from her in an iron chair. He looked at
each of them in turn with his patient, yellow eyes. Pearl watched
him. His eyes were pitiless and serene, like his grandmother's.
Thomas called her name again. He pushed a white mug of coffee
toward her fingers.

I have to stop this, Pearl thought. I'm going mad. Everything was turning white. Her white nails were gnawed and ugly upon the smooth white mug. She had let one of the children paint them. There was the story, wasn't there? about the English-woman, who could have been French or Dutch, or even a wealthy American, with one of those wealthy purses or belts or eyeglass cases that says upon it "shit shit shit shit shit," and this woman, whoever she was, was mad but she had been cured of it and they had asked her what it had been like in there, in madness, and she'd said, the angels are white, they give off the most amazing light . . .

"Please," Pearl said.

The adults stared at her. The children clamored around. Franny was picking the Queen Anne's lace which grew raggedly in the cracks between the bricks. She spread her fingers beneath one and sang:

"Mama had a baby and its *head* popped off!"

The flower sailed into Pearl's lap, where she looked at it.

"Please what, Pearl?" Shelly said.

Pearl sipped at the coffee. "Thank you, rather," she said. It was amazing that they couldn't see what was happening. She looked at the children's dark and lovely and thoughtless little faces. And then again, with great effort, as though she were hauling herself out of a well, she thought, I must stop this. She prayed for something utilitarian and magical to help her out of the well. Reality is so confusing. The senses are such bad witnesses. She could trust none of them.

Sam smiled at her.

Thomas was talking about sea turtles. "The most astonishing thing," he said. "I saw it once in Florida. Hundreds of newly hatched turtles unerringly making their way to the sea beneath the terrible shadows of the gulls."

"The classic example," Lincoln mumbled around mouthfuls of food, "of the spontaneity of the quest for the not-yet-seen."

Florida, Pearl thought. So that's what Thomas had been doing there. He hadn't been sitting around the hospital plotting ways to throttle her at all. He'd been on the beach, like any tourist, watching tiny flippered things gobbled up on their way back home. Things sometimes were more proper than they seemed.

"We must go into town today," Miriam said, "and get the children their presents."

Pearl straightened in her chair. "Yes," she said. "Oh, yes, what should I get, do you think?"

All very well to speak of ordinary things, she thought. But the sun was so hot and her soul was crying out for drink. It was the children's birthday. And something terrible was about to happen.

"The boys get knives," Lincoln said abruptly.

"Knives! Whatever for?"

"To cut things with"—Lincoln laughed—"to cut things off with."

"Oh really," Pearl said with relief, grimacing, "how trite."

Lincoln grinned. He lathered butter on a waffle and began to eat again. He had gained seventy-five pounds since he met Shelly. He was vast and smooth-skinned. Pearl thought of his terrible weight upon Shelly, pressing her down.

Shelly said, "We're all going into town later this morning, Pearl, if you'd like to come with us. All the adults I mean ..."

"Town?" Pearl said. "Oh, I don't know about ... town."

"It might be the last good day of the summer. The signs are for an early fall this year."

"Yes, Pearl," Thomas said, "it would do you good. Let the children fend for themselves."

The children around Pearl smiled at her encouragingly. They possessed a sympathetic and profound belief in her manner, which is not to say that they thought for a moment that this manner offered useful truths to them.

"Come to town with us," Thomas insisted.

"All right," she said. To the children, she said, "I'm off with the grownups today."

They giggled and patted her arm.

"We'll leave in an hour," Thomas said.

After breakfast, Pearl wandered down to the pool, followed by some of the children. The slanted roof of the children's stone house rippled in the sun.

The ground around the pool was dark and a little slippery. A lizard was resting in the head of the sculpture. Pearl could see its slender ocher tail.

"Look at me, Pearl!"

Timmy ran from behind her and somersaulted into the water, the surface furling back like a flower to receive him. Down he went to the very bottom. He held the bottom with his hands. The water swept around him there. It hardly looked like Timmy there. He shot up, triumphant. Water ran in long flat streams down his cheeks.

Ashbel said, "Our Mommy made cakes for us all. They're chocolate and jam. We can eat them all tonight."

"Good," Pearl said.

"She's not sneaking any vegetables into them or anything. Just chocolate and sugar and jam. We can eat them all tonight."

"Good," Pearl said.

Pearl saw a large dark shape in the sky next to the top story of the house. It was dark and yet at the same time seemed lighter than the sky. It was dense and black. It was outside of Sam's room.

She didn't ask the children if they saw it too. What if they didn't? She would be all alone.

A winged light beating on the windows of her little Sam's room. On heavy wings, it left.

"What are you children going to be doing today?" Pearl wondered.

"We'll play and hunt and eat and hide," Tracker said.

"It will be like always," Jane said.

"It's nice here when there's just us," Tracker said.

"And Pearl," Ashbel said. "Just us and Pearl. That's the nicest."
He curved his fingers around her wrist.

CHAPTER THIRTEEN

Pearl rode in silence with the others to the dock. Shelly and Lincoln. Miriam and Thomas. The water was dark, the air warm and still.

There was talk of a tropical storm building up several hundred miles off the Outer Banks. They might get more rain tonight or tomorrow.

Pearl looked into the water. A kingdom of creatures there. Discolored froth pressed against the sides of the dock.

"Ughh," she said, "I hate those bubbles, particularly when the wind brings them up on the lawn."

"Once it was believed that sea froth could impregnate a woman," Thomas said.

She blushed, annoyed. "The things they had to worry about in those days!"

"What days were those?" Thomas asked.

"Oh," she said, "imagine. Everyone a neurotic. And no psychiatrists. No gin."

Thomas smiled. His teeth were white but his breath was slightly bad. He wore a cotton shirt that was very white.

Lincoln, in a desultory way, was trying to net a crab. He jabbed the pole down. The pressure of the current pulled the net sideways. The crab escaped into the image of a rock which Lincoln threw disgustedly away.

About a mile offshore, they saw a deer.

"Oh, the poor thing!" Shelly exclaimed.

The animal's head went under for an instant and then resurfaced.

"I'm so glad the children aren't here to see this. How sad this is," Shelly said.

There was nothing that could be done. The launch was pulled past. The pretty animal's uncomprehending head receded.

Pearl looked back at the shape in the water. It had no sense of its needs, its strangeness, its goneness. It wanted the sea merely, the cold, inaccessible depths. Pearl could understand that. People changed after death, of course, they passed into the interests of another life. It all went on and on and on. We are like salamanders dancing in the fire.

"She looks so determined," Shelly persisted. "Do you think she might make shore?"

"It," Lincoln said irritably. "Animals are referred to as 'it.'"

Thomas said, "You know, ten or twelve people drown off this town each summer."

"It sounds more like a matter of statistics than of death," Lincoln said. He giggled and shrugged.

Pearl leaned back against the boat cushions. The canvas warmed her back. She stretched out her legs and noticed Thomas glance at them.

For quite some time now, Pearl hadn't been able to understand where she had seen the resemblance. But it had certainly been her impression, years before, that Thomas looked like Walker. Perhaps it was that she was just remembering Walker less well. She kept seeing him in a green smoking jacket, for example, that she knew he never had. And his style of lovemaking had seemed inappropriate to her past responses for years now. He would brush against her mind like a moth against a bulb and she would try to think about him. How did he comb his hair ... how did he help a child into a boat ... ? She would try to think of the brief time they shared before Sam was born. But of course one never shares time with anyone. Not even now, this instant now, when she was staring into Thomas' eyes. This moment in the sunlight, with the other shore approaching, meant nothing. We find the ones with whom we can share nothing, that nothing not being time. There Thomas sat, hunched forward slightly, his eyes smiling slightly, massively present and at ease, utterly familiar to her and completely unknown.

The children said that once a teen-age girl had killed herself for love of Thomas. Thomas had been in divinity school at Harvard. After the incident he switched to law. Religion had become too confused with the ethical morality to be of interest to him. Then some other scandal occurred and he dropped that profession as well.

Pearl saw him in an Episcopal skirt, his clipped nails flashing among the little picture wafers, his fingers pressing them down upon lopped tongues. A wicked angel, sexless and a little violent, his eyes burning beneath his bushy brows.

The girl who killed herself had a peculiar name. It was like a name chosen off a perfume bottle, something the girl had chosen herself. Pearl imagined her sitting zipped and trembling in a pew, looking into those smoking eyes of the young interning priest. She imagined the dead girl imagining him before she died, sticking her head in her mother's oven, imagining Thomas doing it to her, doing it with his eyes perhaps, the girl possessed by a florid and exquisite confusion so complete that she could, in fact, ignore the fact that her own shining hair, which she envisioned roped around his fist, was fluffed against bubbles of blackened cheese on the black interior of her mother's Garland.

The unheard cry escapes. She died a virgin. Thomas did it anally perhaps. Perhaps he *did* do it with his eyes. She was confused after all, a flashy piece at fourteen, holding herself together with thin arms. But Thomas had probably done nothing. He was just a handsome man, rich, and at Harvard. He had rich skin. He spoke in gleaming rhythms of bewildering metaphor. He spoke about the highest, unhuman ambitions of man.

She gained access to him by speaking of her brother. The child had sugar. He was sickly. He was miserable, picked his nose and ate it, couldn't say certain words at all, words like "love" and "orange," just *couldn't* say them.

Some things are not essential, Thomas said, denying this nymph, this girl with the carefree name, the joy she craved.

There were two or three Thomases really. The one she saw, the one he was, and the one he would become. She read too much. She'd lie about on Saturdays with her girl friends, reading aloud from their parents' paperbacks ... "Her mouth accepted his turgid organ" ... they'd read and sweat. "... he draped her across the ottoman. He entered her ..." She didn't think it through. She thought she'd be able to hear his comments when he received news of her death. Well, perhaps she did. He made none. He really wasn't nice, although he did take her little brother to the island with him several weekends in a row after the funeral. He took a child sick in spirit and made him well. He suffered little children in the biblical sense. The boy grew up a success.

After Thomas left the university, he began going out with very beautiful women. He'd take them to Newport or Saratoga or even Porto Ercole, but in the end he'd bring them to the island, where they'd poach lobsters for him and listen to him talk in ontological dialects. They were so impressed with the quality of his mind. Really how could one think and speak at the same time ... Amazing when you thought about it. The flow of those ... words. The tumefaction of ... thought. It must have been both exciting and degrading to be with him. Of course, he made enemies. It became too tedious for him to treat his affairs as though they were real. He broke a woman's arm while dancing. He was even married once for four days to a socialite who threw the I Ching. She simply vanished, taking nothing, even leaving her sticks behind. Another woman who knew him well was a novelist. She used Thomas as a figure in her most repellant book. Physically he did not read the same, and it was considered that the perversions practiced were substitutions for those which actually took place.

He was a well-known mystery. He was often sighted in several night clubs at once, or simultaneously walking down Fifth Avenue with an actress or two and having lunch at the Cloister on Sea Island with a seven-foot artist who made hair pictures.

Then he retired. He came to the island where he had spent summers as a child. He restored the house that had been let go. He found that he had a talent for children.

Why was Thomas the way he was about children? He had been doing this for seven, fourteen, twenty-one years now. Hitler's father raised bees. It's in all the histories. But what is to be made of that? Raising bees. Thomas' father was a judge. He had no hobbies, although he did have an extraordinary collection of compasses. He had two sons and, late in life, a daughter. His wife painted plates and took codeine.

Walker said that Thomas was always mysterious about things, even as a child. He had his secrets, and even then had the intellectual's love for the irrational moment, the usurpation of natural law. Once, when he was nine or ten, he found a bicycle washed up on the rocks in that cleft mid-island where the sea beats upon the island's heart. The bicycle was completely plated with oysters. He begged the judge to buy him a life-sized mannequin from one of the stores in the city. He threw it into the sea and dragged it up a few weeks later. The encrusted creation was in his room even today, the children said. The children said he had all sorts of peculiar stuff in his room from all periods of time and stages of man's degradations and hopes. He had a clay statue of Osiris, the flayed God, the mutilated god of regeneration. And over his desk was an Ethiopian tapestry depicting a castration in battle. The enemy looked as though they were smoking cigars.

Thomas was unreasonable with the children, impatient and demanding. He had a strong, unsympathetic face and a quick, eclectic mind. Thomas had a cruel streak. The children said they'd seen it. A pale line running from armpit to hip on one side and from armpit to fingertips on the other, quite visible, hot even, exposed when they didn't please him. He was convinced, quite simply, that their minds were capable of anything. He saw each child as an exhilarating beast of transmutative delights which he could take great pleasure in. Year after year, he taught them. He had found his place in his own life. He spent the years observing and instructing these delightful, innocent, and dangerous creatures. He had no notion that they lied shamelessly to him in their every word and action, not did it occur to him that they would, with the genius he unconsciously had always believed to be finite, refuse to go the way of the other children before them.

He had taken over the island and its history as though it means nothing, as though the present never reshapes the past. He really did not believe in the children, that was it. He didn't believe in them the way Pearl did. Pearl's chin was in her hands. She straightened up. She wondered if she had been asleep. Her lip seemed wet. For some reason, Lincoln was discussing the history of the three-pronged fork. Thomas had slowed the boat in the harbor and voices drifted clearly to her. The day beat down upon them with its intimations of night.

Once, even yesterday, she had thought Thomas was powerful, even perhaps, evil, but now she knew he was as helpless as she was, as they all were now on this day with its night coming. Night runs with its children, Sleep and Death, with its twins, the true dream and the false one.

They pulled alongside the pier in Morgansport. As one barfly said to another: Life is a dirty glass or a very dirty glass. There was red seaweed, a dead crab floating belly-up. An entire page from a newspaper floated past, flat-out and completely readable.

A laconic model with straight, blunt-cut hair was posing in a flowered gown. Pearl touched her own undernourished hair. That's for me, she thought. That's my style. The paper struggled around the boat and drifted off.

Pearl opened her pocketbook and peered inside. There was a fifty dollar bill there. Perhaps she should get her hair done, like the girl floating in the water.

The others were already making plans for returning. It was almost eleven. They would meet back at the pier at three. Pearl stood up uncertainly. She smoothed her dress.

"Are you coming with me, Pearl?" Miriam asked.

"Oh goodness," Pearl said. "It's too early in the day yet for me to make decisions." She laughed as though she had been joking. But she followed the others off the boat and onto the dock, and trailed off after Miriam toward the center of town.

It seemed so peculiar to her to be without the children. In the past, when she had ventured into town, some of them would always be with her. They would come into the liquor store where she ordered her wine and gin. The children selected the bottles with the prettiest labels.

The town was small and busy. The people seemed sharply defined, as though they had great black borders around them. Pearl followed Miriam up and down the aisles of the grocery store, she followed Miriam into and out of bookstores and banks. She stood with Miriam in a long line at the post office. They used Pearl's bag for the mail. Most of it was addressed to Miriam. Envelopes full of swatches of fabric, tearings of silk and lace. Ecru, velvet, denim. Each with its tale of simple betrayal and the tedium of love.

Pearl could never understand why people who did not even know Miriam would want to send her the poor threads of their lives. They never saw the skirts, which were really more like wall tapestries, although they received long letters of advice and thanks. The skirt she was wearing now consisted of nine hundred histories.

Miriam was like a saint dragging herself through the desert with the sins of the world hanging from her waist. Pearl supposed it was all a little crazy on Miriam's part. She was even in possession of a bit of the headband of a woman who had died in climax. It had probably been posted by the lover. Pearl herself had never given Miriam anything for her skirts. Of course, Pearl did not consider that she had anything of her own. Pearl felt that she was renting space here in this life. And it belonged to her no more than to the person who would occupy it next.

Pearl looked in shop windows at suntan lotions and rope brace-lets. She looked into a fenced yard where a woman was weeding. She was going to make an effort, she really was.

"Hello," Pearl said.

They went into a drugstore. Pearl bought candy for the children. She bought Miriam and herself ice-cream cones. She was begin-ning to feel a little better. She bit into her cone and laughed. The cold made her teeth ache.

She looked at kites and bubble bath. She should get them for the children. They would like frivolous things like this. But something in her mind said it was hopeless, it was all hopeless.

She wandered among the aisles. The store seemed overstocked in sanitary napkins. Several shelves of various brands were offered. Pearl found herself standing in front of the shelves in the attitude of one appraising fine jewelry. Lying among the boxes of Tampax was a package of Tarot cards with the picture of the Hanged Man on the cover. Pearl picked it up. She had seen these before. In her childhood . . . in the store of an old lady who ran a market in her home, who kept ducks in pens to be slaughtered. The Hanged Man. Well, he certainly looked peaceful, Pearl thought. She tried to receive intimations concerning her higher nature from the card but couldn't manage to. Wasn't this what was supposed to hap-pen? One was supposed to receive intimations. He certainly looked peaceful, Pearl thought. But dead, she would imagine, although his eyes were open. Well, neither alive nor dead.

"What do you think of this?" Pearl asked Miriam. She had placed the deck of cards back on the shelf where she had found it. She pointed them out to Miriam.

"They don't belong there," a clerk said critically. "They belong in notions. I swear some people have to go out of their way to put something where it doesn't belong." The clerk's face was addressing Miriam while it scolded Pearl. Both women looked at Pearl.

The bottom of Pearl's cone was leaking. She asked the girl behind the soda fountain if she could throw it away. "What is really needed is a drink," she said to no one in particular. But to Miriam she said:

"I think I must sit down for a bit. I'm not used to so much excitement."

Miriam said, "Yes, I have to be some place at one myself."

In the street again, they separated. Pearl hesitated in front of a store which seemed to deal exclusively in plates with asparagus and onions painted on them. A stocky woman in a tee shirt that said A WOMAN WITHOUT A MAN IS LIKE A FISH WITHOUT A BICYCLE stood beside her. Pearl wanted to ask her what it meant but the woman looked fierce and impatient so Pearl didn't. If she inquired, the woman might say something unpleasant. She might call her a simple-witted twat or something.

Pearl walked briskly away in search of a bar. Rattled, she took several turns that took her away from the town's business area and back into cobblestoned, residential streets. She passed a row of lovely eighteenth-century houses. The doors stood open as though to invite adoration. A glimpse within showed glossy floors, linen love-seats, fresh flowers.

" . . . I said lime sherbet to go with the blueberries, not lemon sherbet for christ the fuck's sakes," said a voice from one of the houses. "I loathe lemon sherbet."

A brown Jaguar passed her on the street. It's brake lights reddened. Lincoln pushed his head out.

"Hello, Pearl," he said. "Are you lost?" He laughed. His face was pink and damp. Shelly looked at Pearl and shook her head.

"I was just looking for a bite to eat," Pearl said.

Shelly raised her brows.

"Well, something to eat and drink," Pearl said.

"Get in, get in," Lincoln said. "We'll drive to The Silent Woman. Tables set up beneath the trees. Piccolo music. Quiche appetizers. And an excellent bartender."

Pearl shrugged. She knew Lincoln just wanted to show off his car. She opened the rear door and slid across the seat.

"Walker had a car like this," she said.

"No, that was a Mercedes. You've still got that, you know. It's still garaged down there by the dock."

"I don't know anything about cars. It smelled like this one."

Lincoln laughed. "I've had this for over a year and haven't driven it more than half a dozen times. It costs me two thousand dollars every time I turn on the ignition." He sounded delighted.

Pearl said nothing. She slumped in the back seat, pretending she was the female wanted on the post office posters, captured now and being taken to a maximum-security prison.

The car stopped before a small white house with a large and quite beautiful garden. A sign on the gate post said THE SILENT WOMAN. Pearl gazed out at it unhappily. Nevertheless, there was a man in shirt sleeves and a madras vest behind a table that held a great many bottles.

"It's a proper place, Pearl," Shelly said. "You don't want to go into a bar all by yourself. You've got to think about these things."

"Are you sure an invitation isn't necessary there?" Pearl asked.

"No, no."

Pearl got out of the car. "Well," she said, "thank you."

The car moved creamily off.

She did not want to go in right away. The bartender looked at her impassively and slowly inserted his little finger in his ear and pushed it about.

Across the street was an abandoned church, metamorphosed into a community center. There was the sound of vacuum cleaners and the muted barks of dogs. A bulletin board banged into the shaggy grass announced a puppet show at noon. THE MAGIC PAPER BEASTS LIVE PUPPETS LIFE SIZED BRING YOUR OWN MUSIC BRING YOUR OWN SELVES. An elongated papier-mâché object was draped over the bulletin board. It was an angel-type creature with hectic cheeks and yellow yarn hair hanging down like donkey ears.

Puppet shows had always been associated in Pearl's mind with audiences of well-bred children and competent mothers who knew how to raise their children properly. She sighed, looking at the church. It was a simple Protestant structure. The stained-glass windows depicted mountains, trees and stars. She could imagine it inside. The pews latched, the carpeting a muddy brown, the abandoned pulpit, pine.

Behind her, in the garden, a man's voice said:

"I have two kids by my third wife and you've never seen such pampered horrors. Bills, pills, anorexia nervosa. Number Three always believed in making a grand occasion out of everything. She'd give them a party on Mother's Day. Now, Number Two never had kids. She was cuckoo, you know. She kept the wine and threw away the roses, as they say."

Pearl could smell liquor on the air.

"Another tequila sunrise," the man's voice said.

Oh it was so gay and civilized, Pearl thought, in this summer resort, this last resort. So gay and civilized to drink on a summer's day beneath the trees. To drink drinks that had names, that were your friends.

Her fingertips felt icy. No, she must not drink. She must keep a sober witness. Had she so quickly forgotten the hellish convictions she had held?

This is no kind of life, Pearl thought.

She walked across the street to the church. Just within the open front door was a wooden baptismal font holding a silver bowl. The bowl was, strangely enough, filled with water. The church was empty except for a small child seated behind a card table.

"You might as well come in free," the child said. "I guess no one else will be arriving."

Pearl hesitated. The church was warm and smelled sweet as though small things had died between its walls. With what forms of resurrection had the faithful found comfort here? Gone now. The faithful were being faithful somewhere else. There was an electric hot plate at the back of the nave with a long extension cord plugging it into the wall.

"You don't want to perform just for me, do you?" Pearl asked. "Please don't feel you have to do that."

"We don't mind," the child said. "You can sit down anywhere."

It seemed peculiar to Pearl to be speaking with a child not her own. Or rather, not her own, but of the family of children who . . .

"Yes," she said. "I'll sit down."

Pearl chose the very last pew. She stared at the front of the church. Suddenly she twisted around and said, "Do you know Sam? He's my child. He's my little boy."

"What does he look like? Have you lost him?" The child kept his mouth open after he had stopped speaking.

"Why no . . . I mean . . . no."

"I think I know him," the child said.

Pearl turned around again. There was a huge cardboard backdrop on what now could only be considered a stage, supported by twin lecterns. The cardboard was painted and cut out to depict a nighttime scene of moon and stars. There was also a two-dimensional bed drawn on the left.

Beside Pearl, on a gray wall, was an imprint of a cross. Like a scar upon the dust. A legend that no longer satisfied.

Something cavorted past her down the aisle. It looked like a gigantic tooth with a large gray hole in it. This was followed by other forms, wrapped in antique clothes and encased in papier-mâché heads. An apple ran down, followed by a repulsive-looking worm, the worm being an energetic child crawling in a brown sack. On the stage a large boy puppet with a featureless cloth head and spindly cloth limbs was being moved about by means of a stick shoved beneath its shirt. A person dressed all in black with a black-hooded head held the stick and crouched on the floor, flipping and flopping the puppet around, while a voice from somewhere went on and on in a muted, indistinguishable way, speaking of childhood, obedience, bad dreams and robbers.

Pearl sat with a sad tight smile upon her face. It seemed that nothing could be done these days on a strictly human level. Her thoughts began to wander. She missed the children. She wished she had a baby of her own. She liked babies, the way they felt your face with their hands, the way they put their fingers in your mouth as though they were putting them in their own . . .

The voice, which sounded like a scratchy recording, continued its blurred axioms from a loudspeaker above her.

Another creature had arrived on the stage, some sort of flying insect with wire antennae and a large orange sun painted on its back. Its face, which looked like that of a woman, was heavily made-up. And its belly was huge. Really, Pearl thought, why was a woman that pregnant tearing around in such an absurd production? Perhaps it was supposed to be a spider. And what was that that was told about spiders . . . they were the images of women who had hanged themselves . . .

Pearl yawned nervously. The whole production was harmless and exuberant enough but the thought that it was being enacted expressly for her made her feel uncomfortable. She felt a little disgusted. She might as well be drunk, she thought.

She slipped out of the pew and backed into the street. She went directly into the garden of The Silent Woman where she ordered a very dry martini. She drank. Her fingers with their shattered, uneven nails held the glass. The rind floated there like a sliver of moon. She ordered another.

CHAPTER FOURTEEN

The people around Pearl were eating. Someone was eating squab, another liver, a third soft-shelled crabs. The smell of the food nauseated Pearl.

Overhead something settled in a tree. Shadows passed across the grass. She looked up into the sky and saw large thin clouds moving across the sun. Sunlight flowed across her table again and then leapt onto the grass, traveling to a picket fence where a shirtless young man in wide purple trousers like a gangster's was painting the weathered wood white.

A woman on Pearl's left swallowed a spoonful of something red and white. She said, "He goes into Mass. General on Monday. A brain tumor." She put the spoon down and opened her handbag that was in the shape of a house, painted with windows and doors. She took a magazine out of the little house and folded it back to a page with large print, an illustrated page.

"It's not done every day, of course, but it's not uncommon. The operation is described very well in here," she said. "I can't explain it very well myself but the *Reader's Digest* does a wonderful job. I swear by the *Digest*. I haven't missed a month in fifteen years. He's dismayed about it, of course, but it has to be done. You'd be surprised how many people have to have it done."

"The young man that time in Texas, the one who shot everybody, didn't he have one of those tumors?" the other woman said. "That young man on that tower?"

There was forever a little sober person inside Pearl somewhere, overhearing conversations, and one of these days, just before the light perhaps, she knew it was going to rise up and strangle her, the little sober person being no friend.

Across the street, the Magic Paper Beasts had left the church and were assembled on the lawn. Pearl felt a little better about them now. The drinks had brightened her perceptions considerably. They certainly were life-sized. An energetic troupe, elaborately costumed, wearing those plaster heads. One of them, an odd mixture of lion and cheerleader, dashed over to the garden and peered over the fence at the people there. It was made up to be quite ferocious but it had jolly mittened hands and a humorous, inviting manner. However, what it was inviting them to do was not quite clear. It did not seem to want the people to follow it to the church lawn, or, in any way, to become part of the production. It did not even want money. It waved away several proffered bills. The diners tittered as it lingered there, not quite harassing them, a crude and childish construction and not in its first appearance by any means. The paper cheek was slightly squashed and was leaking a powdery substance and the paint was faded as though it had been stored in the sun.

It ignored Pearl, no doubt insulted by her impolite departure. Behind its eyes, which were raggedly carved holes, Pearl detected other eyes, small and not quite lined up with the holes. Were they the eyes of a man or a child? There was the smell of sweat coming from the figure.

It finally loped away. The others went back to their food, but Pearl began watching the activity on the lawn, grasping it quite well now, she thought.

The figures were outlandish personifications of a child's dreams and fears. They were animals and pieces of cake. They were toys and snakes. They were the dull admonishments and threats of the adult world. The child that dreamed writhed on the grass that had become his bed. He jerked and tossed, manipulated by the boy in black. All those things leaping and creeping around him were only the products of the dreamer's exhausted imagination, although in visible fact, the dreamer was the only performer who was a fabrication, being moved about by the stick as he was. The black-suited boy who did the manipulations, sometimes flat on his stomach, sometimes on his haunches, even, like a dog, on his back, amused Pearl. The device was so highly visible, so intrusive that she stared at it, entranced. There was the Shadow, brighter than day, guiding and controlling, the star of the show.

The troupe wasn't attracting much of an audience. A few children gaped at it from the street and then moved off. Actually, it might seem frightening to children, Pearl thought. Not suitable. All that. Yet what was suitable for children? Impressionable little lumps of clay that they were.

The woman on Pearl's left was now eating something brown. Pearl heard her companion say, "We were playing that dreadful game Diplomacy with the Joneses and the Foleys and the Prinns, and John got up and went out with Penny for one of those diplomacy periods, you know, where they haggle for supply centers. John had Turkey, and Penny, the bitch, had Austria-Hungary, and they were gone for one half hour, which was acceptable enough as far as the rules of the game went but when they came back John had a stain on his pants the size of goddamn England and I just left. Like that I left. I walked out of that goddamn room with her goddamn *crudités* and her goddamn fake brick and I called my lawyer and I've been a happy woman ever since."

Pearl twisted slightly in her seat away from them. A man was standing in front of her, facing her, looking into the garden, blocking her view. He looked familiar. There are some people who look familiar to you only when you're drunk, she thought. The man was speaking to her. She realized it was Thomas.

She interrupted him, "Do you see that person in black over

there, pretending to be invisible?"

He turned, "No," he said.

Pearl giggled.

"Why don't we go somewhere and have some lunch?" he said.

"All right," she said, still giggling.

"We can eat right in the main house here. They have a good dining room. Quieter. We'll have bouillabaisse."

Pearl looked at him. He was wearing a pale suit and a dark blue shirt. His tie was a school tie of some sort, with small signs or heads embossed upon it.

"You changed your clothes," she said.

He shrugged. "I just bought them. I felt that I needed a new suit."

She started to giggle again but gulped it back.

"Laughter indicates a healthy view of the world, Pearl. I'm glad to see you so well."

Pearl came out of the garden and they went up the wide, pleasant steps of the house. They entered a dim hall with painted black floors. To the right were several closed doors and to the left a large room set up with tables. A fireplace was filled with an arrangement of sea grasses.

Pearl's heel slipped on an uneven board and she staggered into the room.

"Goodness, it's dark in here," she said. "Why is it so dark in here?" she said. "Have they been throwing up on the table cloths?"

"I'll order for us," Thomas said. He went off, out into the hallway again. Pearl unfolded her napkin and placed it on her lap. She waited. Waited as a child waits for an adult, as an animal waits, without meditation or exception.

Thomas returned with two wine glasses and an uncorked bottle of wine.

"Well," Pearl said, "this is very nice." She wasn't at all hungry.

But she felt elated. It seemed a fateful moment and she wished that the children were here to distract her from its implications. But obviously it was improper for her to think that a child could save her. Improper to think that a child could offer her any salvation whatsoever. Little children were too innocent to provide salvation. Indeed, little children were always leading their elders right into the teeth of death.

"Have you had a pleasant day?" Thomas inquired politely. He poured.

"I don't like town much. I don't know, I can do without the town. It's good to know though that life goes on. Over here, I mean, I suppose." The wine in the glass rocked up, wetting her fingers. "It tried to do some shopping for the children, for their birthday, but there was nothing that seemed right."

"There's nothing that they need. They have everything in their heads. They give little things to one another, as you might remember. Things they've found or made themselves."

"Oh yes, " Pearl said, "they *are* resourceful."

On the wall Pearl could now make out a painting of the moon in its last phase. The horned moon . . . She saw Thomas raise his arm and slowly push the arm across toward her. He brushed something off her blouse with his hand. Her breasts tingled.

"When children kiss, they bite," Pearl said. "I was amazed when it happened the first time. When they kiss, they take out little heart-shaped bites."

"That's just metaphor," Thomas said.

Pearl sipped her wine. It was cold and tasted like flowers.

"Sometimes," she said softly, "I think I'd like to have another child. Seven years seems so long. It seems that everything happened so long ago. I would be better with him, you know? I mean, he would be a comfort to me. Not that Sam is a bad boy, I'm not saying that. I'm not saying he's a problem at all." Her mind was racing. She leaned forward intently. "He's not special, I'm not saying that. He's just like the others. Well, that's not quite right. He's not as wild as some of the others. He's more ordinary if anything. And I'm glad. When he was born, after he was born and Walker died, I worried . . . I was so confused . . . well it ruined my life, as you know. But I realize . . ." Pearl had forgotten her point. Her mind was racing across the water to the children waiting for her to return. She looked at Thomas with perplexity and said loudly, ". . . realize that he's just a sunny little boy, a calm and ordinary little boy, and I wish you would leave him alone."

"Leave him alone?"

"Yes," she said, swallowing.

"You talk as though I'm a modern-day Faust. I have no unutterable secrets, no black powers."

"Faust?" Pearl said. Her voice sounded thick to her ears.

"Faust ended his days beaten up by devils and buried in horse shit," Thomas said easily. "I deserve better than that, don't I?"

Pearl chuckled. She was amazed at herself.

Thomas said, "The pact I've signed has been with myself alone."

"Oh a pact, really. That's pretentious a bit. I mean, really, don't you think?" Pearl said unhappily.

"I thought it was a term you would appreciate. It's obvious you've made your own arrangements. You realize that children respect madness so you've taken the role yourself of their holy fool."

Pearl wasn't listening. She watched Thomas as he pushed the tie so that it fell within his jacket.

The fish soup arrived. The waiter served it from a large tureen. Pearl looked down into the soup, at the beads of butter and saffron swirling there. An eyelash floated down. She removed it with her fingertip.

"It must be diet," she said. "My eyelashes. They fall out all the time. And it takes nine months to make a new one."

The glasses here were not dirty. Neither was the silverware. Everything was very clean.

"I'm sick," Pearl said suddenly.

"You quarrel with your sickness," Thomas said calmly. "Everyone has a sickness. It should be cared for but not cured."

"What?" Pearl said dully. She wished that he would pour more wine. Thomas' way of talking made her dizzy.

"I said, each of us has a sickness. It is not something that should be cured. To eradicate the sickness would be to eradicate the self."

"Honestly," she said, rousing herself, "what a lot of trash you talk." She looked at him restlessly. She felt poised on the brink of something terrific.

He filled her glass by half. She curled her fingers around it but did not drink.

"I have never understood," she said, "how it happened anyway. Everyone acts as though they know, but I don't know." More people fucked with the Devil than they did with the Lord. Wasn't that why nuns covered up their ears? But that wasn't the answer. "Do you know?" she demanded.

"Yes," he laughed.

"There were animals," Pearl said. "And then there were subhumans and animals and then there was that incredible change, that catastrophe, and then there were human beings."

"A random phenomenon occurring when a vital urge was aroused."

"But it didn't evolve," Pearl said. "It just happened. There wasn't time for it to evolve. There never would be enough time."

"A species under great pressure or in great need producing acausal changes in its material form."

"You don't know," Pearl sighed.

"Visitors from another planet caused the change," Thomas suggested. "Sin did. Through sin we became human and different."

"What was our sin?" Pearl whispered.

"A repellant sexual fantasy," Thomas smiled. "The cause of it all. Yes, the most disgusting sexual fantasy of all lent itself better than any other to the formulation of the most spiritual ideas of which the mind is capable."

He was laughing at her. She bit her lip and watched him eat.

"It was separating ourselves from the animals," she said. "That was the sin."

"Oh Pearl," he said. "Relax and enjoy your meal."

"I have never known ..." she began, and stopped. Then she drank her wine at once and went on hurriedly, "I'm glad I had a child but it's not a question of being able to do something, actually, is it? It's not like being able to make an omelet, even. I'd love to be able to make an omelet, even that. Fluffy but runny inside and all folded over in a piece. Because it doesn't matter if it tastes good. If it tastes good and it isn't presented well, it's a failure. I mean, anyone can eat eggs right, that's not my point ..."

Thomas put his fingers to her lips. They were so warm. It was a terrible sensation. She wanted to close her eyes.

"Sssshh," he said.

She pulled back. "Oh, I'm drunk, aren't I?" she said. "It's such a good idea to have a few drinks in the afternoon before one has to start drinking at night, but now I'm afraid I'm drunk ... it's just my fate to be a drunk."

"Fate, Pearl." He shook his head.

"The demands of living have consequences," Pearl said carefully, "and that is called fate."

"Fate is vulgar." Thomas dipped some bread into his soup. He ate. Pearl watched him.

"Even in my dreams, I'm drunk," she said.

"St. Augustine thanked God for not making him responsible for his dreams."

"I'm not responsible for anything as far as I can tell," Pearl said.

She watched him eat, the soft sea flesh entering his mouth.

"Everything is sex," Pearl sighed. "To dream of someone or to want to go somewhere. Eating is sex and music is sex ... What is childhood a preparation for ... I mean, those poor children ..."

"Do you know what Jesus did when he was a boy? Do you know what he did to the children who would not play with him?"

Pearl's elbow bumped the soup.

"He turned them into goats."

"Oh," Pearl exclaimed. "Into kids! It's a joke you've told me. Children into kids! That's not in the Bible."

"Do you know that parents told their children to shun the child Jesus because he was a sorcerer? He played by the river and he would mould shapes of animals out of the mud, and he was able to make the animals walk away from him and he was able to command them to return. And once he formed twelve sparrows out of clay and let them fly away."

"Well that sounds right, I guess. I suppose if he were a child he would be going around doing things like that."

"Several times he caused children who quarreled with him to die. Joseph said to Mary, 'We should not allow him to go out of the house for everyone who displeases him is killed.' He killed a teacher once who whipped him."

"Oh," Pearl said earnestly, "that must have been another child who did those things, don't you think?"

"Why do you say that?"

"Jesus was supposed to be charitable, wasn't he? And good? 'The joyous boy of the fields.' I mean, he sounds like a little bastard." She laughed. The laugh sounded like a chain dropped upon the floor.

"You're not eating," Thomas said.

"Is there something sweet I can have? I'm afraid this doesn't appeal to me much."

Thomas called the waiter. There was cake. He brought Pearl cake in a puddle of cream. She sampled the cream with her finger.

"I don't believe Jesus was ever a child anyway," Pearl said, "I mean in that sense."

"It's true," Thomas nodded. "The figures that changed our histories had lives based on special knowledge, on a physicality of spirit that had nothing to do with their shapes as men."

"I don't . . . I wouldn't know about that. I don't . . ."

He smiled at her indulgently. He seemed to have white spokes radiating from his eyes. Pale etchings in his sun-tanned face.

"I don't see why you want to talk with me," Pearl said.

"It's true that the feminine character doesn't interest me much. Most women use a combination of enthusiasm and ignorance to get through their days."

Pearl poured a glass of wine for herself. "The children told me about your room," she said. "They told me that you have a jock strap hanging on the wall with a rat in it."

"That object appeared in a highly successful show at the Museum of Modern Art in New York," Thomas said, nonplused.

Pearl swabbed up more cream with her finger.

Thomas said, "The feminine character interests me quite a bit actually."

"Too late to be interested in my character," she said. "Poor Pearl's character is just about gone." She was having a terrific rush. She was hearing everything but not listening much. Her mind was smooth and sunny. The children were calm. The animal was still.

"I used to dislike you," she said cheerfully. "Now it doesn't matter much."

"You lead a charmed life," he said.

"I once fell down the steps coming to dinner," Pearl said. "It's true. How many steps, thirty-seven or . . . and I didn't break a thing."

"If you were lost in a blizzard, you would probably be taken in by wolves."

It didn't last long, the blossoming, the rush, the flying. She smiled.

"It's a great gift to be a survivor," Thomas said. "I try to impress upon the children how important a gift it is. I'd like to think that if anything happened to me the children would be successful in their own society, that they would not need the false securities of . . ."

"It's a funny phrase, isn't it, 'if anything happened'? People use it all the time, don't they? All kinds of people, as though it meant a lot of things when actually it only means one."

Pearl picked up a utensil beside her plate and pushed it into the cake. She raised a piece of cake to her lips and secured it safely in her mouth. She was startled at the feel. She slid the runcible spoon distastefully past her lips. Who had ever invented that neither-nor arrangement? She went back to picking at the cake with her fingers.

"You're not a bad man," Pearl said, as though to herself, "you've loved all those children for all these years."

"Oh, to be quite frank, I'm not sure it's love. It's an interest, certainly. Children have always fascinated me. The energy that shapes and moves them is not the same as ours."

The children stirred in Pearl's mind. They raised their heads.

"But then they grow," Thomas was saying. "They become imprisoned in their bodies. They acquire their faces. It's unfortunate, really."

"Well," Pearl said, "children grow. That's what they do. It's practically their sole occupation."

"Yes, yes," he said eagerly. His face seemed to be widening before her. Wine splashed upon her wrist.

"It's only in childhood that life gives you time to confront your soul, your protector, and you see it alive, exactly as it is," Thomas said. "But children grow, as you say. They change. The metamorphosis comes unbidden. They exchange the knowledge of the child for the conventions of the adult, and everything is lost in the transition. Everything. Life itself."

Pearl watched his large, rapacious hands move as he spoke. Everything was an artifice. What the mind thought and the tongue spoke and the heart felt. She watched him in a heavy, sleepy way.

"Man's reason has made him nature's freak," Thomas said.

It was terrible the way he spoke, in that strange, punishing way. She wondered how the children could be so patient and submissive and untouched by him.

"The dichotomy between the anti-world and the world he is forced to experience consume him. The result is death. Such a dichotomy isn't necessary."

"Death isn't necessary?" Pearl said.

"'Death' is a poor word. Merely a means of communicating a memory, a shared experience. Yes, a very poor word, like 'love.'" He rolled the word in his mouth as though it were an oyster, a clot of phlegm.

"You're not experimenting or anything with those children, are you?" Pearl demanded loudly.

Thomas looked at her. He rolled up his napkin and pulled it slowly through his fist. It was a provocative gesture, Pearl thought. She had the shakes. She felt as though she were twitching all over.

"Pearl, you must stop thinking of me as some sort of wizard."

"Well, what are you saying then . . . I mean . . . it's just words you're saying then isn't it? Please, I don't want to talk anymore. Order another bottle of wine, please. Why do you use so many words? Those poor children . . ."

"But you asked me about the children. They have had every freedom. Their fantasies have been encouraged and respected. Some of them are brilliant. Some of them enjoy encyclopedic knowledge. But this is unimportant. It appeals to me far less than it once did. Childhood is the conscious world as well as being the transcendent one. The increase in consciousness is the key to everything. It is the major force of change, a force powerful enough to alter the primitive structures of human instincts and needs. Observing those children over the past few years, I have become an enthusiastic synergist . . ."

"I don't know what that means," Pearl wailed. "Please," she said.

She looked at his tie, at the figures on the tie. They were birds, flying at her from a great distance, not even birds, more the shadows of birds.

"They're just children," she said. "You must not talk to me this way. I don't want to talk about them. I don't want to talk about Sam. I'm not . . . why do you want me to be sick, to be crazy? There's something I know. I knew it a long time ago in my mother's house, in my mother and father's house a long time ago when we were all alive. There was a picture on the wall. It was a woman, a woman, about my age now, and it said underneath her in great scrolly letters 'The Bruised Reed He Will Not Break' and she was obviously in great distress, this poor woman in a long gown and she was embracing a tree. She was spread out on the ground in distress embracing a tree which was not a living tree but sort of a trunk stripped of bark. A terrible-looking thing, all flayed and solid-enough-looking but not giving any comfort to that poor woman as far as I could see and I remember thinking, even as a child, I bet He breaks bruised reeds all the time . . ."

She watched the birds flying toward her, straight toward her eyes.

"I am a bruised reed," she said.

"I'm sorry, Pearl, I've tired you." He reached across the table and stroked her hand. She didn't move her hand away. She dropped her eyes to the roll basket where a fly moved daintily among the crumbs.

"I want to ask you something," she said. "I just want you to answer it in a simple fashion, please. It's just a simple question."

"Of course."

"Is there an old woman who lives in the house? A very old woman?"

"No," Thomas said.

"You're sure?" Pearl said. "You haven't forgotten or anything? Your grandmother or something? This happens occasionally. I've read accounts. People in a big house, they just forget sometimes, and there is this elderly relative living upstairs, living along very frugally, darting in and out of the past, strangling pigeons for her supper or something."

"No," Thomas said.

"She's very old," Pearl said. "Sometimes she hardly looks like an old woman at all. She looks like some bird. A dreadful, fierce bird, like a hawk or . . . when I look at her sometimes it's hard for me to doubt that she's a bird, I see her so clearly. But, after all, I see her and see that it isn't a bird, because as I see her I have the impression that it's an old woman and someone I've been seeing for quite a while now . . ."

"Come, Pearl." Thomas was smiling. "It's all right. You know what that is. It's just the drinking. It's when you've had too much."

"It isn't," Pearl said. She slid her hand away from his.

"Michelet says that birds are 'beneficent cressets of living fire through which the world passes.'"

"I . . . why do you do that? What is that anyway? You answer everything with words, somebody else's words . . . you don't have any of your own . . ."

"Michelet refers to the bird as the agent of purification, 'the wholesome accelerator of the interchange of substances.'"

"I don't know this . . . is he French? He's talking about vultures. Scavengers. I am talking about . . . I don't know . . ."

She rose abruptly. "We all get scared as we get older, I guess that's all it is."

"Dread is a fearful enchantment," Thomas said.

"Those are someone's words too, aren't they?" Pearl cried.

The words were like insects on the walls of the room. Insects, changing colors, fading and shifting and loosing themselves in the room.

"Let's go back to the boat, Pearl. I shouldn't have gone on as I did with you, forgive me."

He spoke in a humorless, unknowing way.

They left the inn and walked out into the street. The sky was queerly bright. The day was stifling.

"Perhaps we'll get some of that storm. Have to get home now, Pearl, batten down the hatches."

He spoke to her as one would a pet on a leash. She followed him miserably. The drinks had let her down. She thought of the children waiting for them, back there, on the other side. She walked very slowly. People hurried past them. She had tried, hadn't she? She was sick of trying to reason things out, of talking. The people hurried past with their huge faces. The world that lured people on was just a prank, didn't they see? Everything could be reversed in an instant. Life could taste like flowers, like the expensive wine that Thomas had bought, but in the end you'd be sick with it.

Lincoln and Miriam and Shelly were waiting at the dock. There were several cartons of bright, cheap toys. Pearl looked at them with effort. Whatever would the children do with those? She lowered herself into the boat.

Thomas cast off the lines. The launch pulled out into the harbor. The sun was shining messily through skinny threads of clouds.

Lincoln was eating a chocolate bar and tying knots into a piece of line. Impossible knots. Who could escape them? He shook his wrist and the line snapped straight.

Off to the west, where the sun rolled, there was a cluster of boats, circling, small boats with the stars of police upon their white sides, making flowers, shifting, backing off, making the stems of flowers. They were bringing something up with hooks.

Miriam took the mail from Pearl's bag and was looking through it.

"What's that?" Shelly asked. She fiddled with the chain around her neck.

"This woman claims that vegetables were the world's first saviors," Miriam said, pressing a letter written in brown spidery ink upon her knees. "She is from North Dakota and she writes, 'against this irrespirable air which first enveloped the earth, vegetables were its saviors,' and she has enclosed a weaving of vegetable fiber that includes the stalks of twenty-three vegetables."

She held up a small faded square, dry and shrunken. She tucked it back into its envelope and unfolded another letter.

"Now here's a woman who has sent me a piece of her son's diaper. She claims that when the diaper was placed across her dead sister's face, the woman began to speak."

"You mean she came back to life?" Pearl asked.

"No, she just began to speak."

"What did she say?" Thomas asked.

There were several moments of silence while Miriam read the letter further. "She writes that her sister said, 'It was not Denny who pushed me, it was a coronary that made me fall.'"

"Why did they put a diaper over her face?" Pearl asked.

"I don't know." Miriam's face was sad and defeated.

"They must have suspected something," Pearl said.

"You are too literal about things," Miriam said.

CHAPTER FIFTEEN

The children were nowhere to be seen when they got back to the house. The doors were open. There was silence.

"They could be anywhere," Thomas said.

"I'm going down to the pool and just sit in it," Shelly said, pushing her hair away from her neck, "I've never been so sticky."

The house seemed cooler. Miriam went immediately to the kitchen, Thomas to his room. Lincoln took a beer from the refrigerator and went down to the sauna.

Pearl went slowly up the stairs. She looked in each one of the children's rooms, but there was no one. No figures bouncing on the bed as there might have been, holding out their arms remorselessly. No one. She hesitated outside the door of her own room. There on the hall floor was a huge construction made of wooden blocks. The children were always building places for themselves. Pearl looked down into it. It had no roof and was a rage of static activity with everything out of scale. A plastic pineapple dwarfed a cloth doll in a crib. A cricket box perched on a fireplace made of small stones. Everything was fashioned in such a way as to represent something it was not. Rugs were made of colored paper. Books were made of stamps. Outside was the mirror sea.

Pearl went into her room and sat on the faded chaise before the window. Her head felt penetrated by slender, silver needles. She made herself a drink. She wanted to make her bones blossom, a different sort of life. The bones blossoming like the flowering wands. An image like the Hanged Man on the tarot cards. As a girl she had preferred the flowering wands, but they signified hope and there was no hope.

She could see the shape of Shelly far away swimming back and forth in the pool.

Without the children, she would be all alone. It would be dreadful. She looked around the room, at the bed with its thin coverlet. Everything happened so long ago. It had always been the past she had tried to remember, but she'd found that the past changes like everything else. It doesn't stay the same. The hunter on the screen shot the bird from the tree but there was another hunter, soaring high up above the world, seeing the patterns and the bones and the lights of things. A hunter with a hunter's eye, flying in the narrow but endless channel between one's death and another.

Outside, the sky swept by in clouds, a great sea of dissolution, harmonious with her thoughts. Yellow and swift and gray, a sick and angry sea. And her mind joined with it without a struggle. Once she had had a baby. He had made nice sounds, night sounds, water sounds. Once she'd had a baby that hadn't been hers.

Pearl went downstairs and poured herself another drink. In the kitchen Miriam had supper on the stove. She sat at the table drinking tea. Pearl looked at her hands on the teacup. Her skin had begun growing over her wedding ring, as the bark of a tree grows over something alien that had been driven into it.

"Why don't you go get the children, Pearl? They must be in their playhouse. It's as though they want to miss their own birthday. I've rung the bell but not a single one's come up."

Pearl looked dreamily out the window where the sky now seemed the color of plums. The last light was collecting in the windows, which seemed inches thick.

Miriam looked at Pearl sternly, but there was no way she could enter Pearl's locked universe. "You're always drinking, you've always got a glass in your hand . . ." she said.

Pearl raised her rather thick eyebrows. "I'll get the children."

"On second thought ..." Miriam began. She stared at Pearl. "It's not right," she said.

Pearl looked at the wedding band sunken into Miriam's flesh. Like her mother's hand. They had to cut the ring off her mother's hand. She never got a new one. Pearl felt the familiar swelling rising in her throat which meant she could cry if she wanted to. Everyone was lonely, so lonely, and everyone longed for that which they had lost and for which there was no hope of ever possessing again.

She felt the hair rise on the back of her neck. She imagined a bat hovering over her head, fanning her with its peculiar little wings. The air around her was comforting, rhythmical and cold. She was so tired, so weary of witnessing, responding. There is no room in life for decorum! At times it is necessary to expose the skeleton within us, to make manifest the death within us!

"Don't be annoyed with me," Pearl said suddenly. "I know about memory too. It's what keeps the others alive, familiar. It's forgetting them that is the second death, the real death." She saw horror fatten Miriam's face. "Oh, I'm sorry," Pearl cried. She ran outside. The earth gnawed at her feet and the wind at her hair. She felt as heavy as the earth and as eternal and indifferent. She should have said ... the dead don't come back because it's less lonely there than here ... it's the only comfort they can give us ... She should have said ... this is it, this is the evening of the day. Our souls are being gathered for the judgment.

The sun was still in the sky along with the moon. The sea seemed higher than the land. Pearl walked toward the stone house, expecting to find the children there. Would they take her with them? Could she be like one of them? She hoped so. The animal was inside her too, the little animal curled around her heart, the beast of faith that knew God.

She put her empty glass upon the grass. Pearl's empty glasses were everywhere, on the beach and in the woods, on the stones that had fallen from the walls.

She put one foot after another on the cool, slippery steps that plunged down into the damp floor of the stone house. She waved an arm about tentatively and then withdrew it, not because it connected with anything, but because it felt as though it had been thrown down a well. She felt in a sock, in a casing, in one of Aaron's animal skins, inside out, her eyes in her flesh. There was an odor here. This was where the meat had been stored long ago. In the winter, living animals had been kept here as well. The room jogged downward, like a theater or a crypt, and its feel suggested other rooms, other levels. One could not scrub the smell of death out of things. The dead had once been here below, in clean cold rooms, and the living above, in warm and troubled waiting.

Light sifted through the dirty glass above. The pitch of the roof met the ground and the still grass glittered in the lower panes. The grass looked sleek as though there was knowledge in it of a storm. She felt the old despair, the old thirst. She was alone, one, and the storm was outside, undifferentiated, everything. She feared and despised her life. She had never wanted this responsibility, this dreadful responsibility to one's own life, the knowledge that everything was outside oneself.

She leaned against the walls, walls that exposed wide ribs beneath the most delicate skin of plaster. She could see more clearly now. She could distinguish the table upon which the carvings stood like shadows. She moved farther into the room, holding the wall.

"Tracker," she called.

He would come to her, wouldn't he? If she called? He was so rough and gloomy, but gentle somewhere in his hunger, scrupulous, brave.

"Ashbel," she called, "Franny . . ." They would come surely if they heard. They were fond of her. They would tumble across her feet and climb her sides and sing their sad songs in her ear with happy voices.

"Trip!" she called, not really expecting him to approach. Him with his grin and his long face, his clever lope, his counterfeit hands . . .

The earth raised up slightly beneath her feet, a mound of fertile earth, suckering weeds. Elevated now, Pearl's fingers grazed the rusting hooks that lined the uppermost part of the walls. She drew her hand back with distaste and sat down. She could not sort out the sounds she heard. Ice settling in a cocktail glass? Someone stirring in a gnawed stall? Music somewhere playing, music both intelligible and untranslatable . . .

No, there was nothing. They were all gone, and she was too. It was so. It had happened. People try living without knowing what it is they're supposed to be doing, and then one is changed and it is over. There is one side and there is the other. And one travels back and forth and it becomes simply too much to bear, the moving back and forth between advent and farewell. Skimming on the surface of the darkness, past the rocks black with mussels, over the shoals and the dead caves full of light, through the race, running, past the buoys that marked safety and danger both, and into the others' harbor. Red, right, return . . . but she was gone from that now. It was over. The town with its faces, with its people talking. Humans have cruel eyes. The eyes of the boy in the animal's head outside the garden in which she drank . . . The eyes of the woman in the drugstore replacing the cards. There was another card on the deck she remembered. The fool followed by the hound. The fool, she was the fool, and yet the edge beneath the fool which opened on the depths held no terror . . .

Pearl heard a noise.

"Jane," she called. "Timmy!"

Her bones creaked as she turned. How she had aged with these children! Her thighs had slackened, her hair had grayed. Her hands trembled as she ate. She could not eat. She could not remember eating.

She could see the dried plants hanging from the window frames, tied by their roots, resting, waiting to be redeemed. She could make out the tubs, nests, bins, the labyrinthe runs. A hundred hiding places here, a hundred homes. Crypt and changing room the same, here. And the yawning womb within her was the room outside she was in, fetid greenhouse or cold grave, sloping out of darkness into a darkness deeper still, into heavy, depleted air.

A quilted light rose and fell in the room. Soundless lightning. A pair of buttocks floated down upon her face like a pale valentine. She could see the wooden animals on the table, disclosed in a circle, knowing no ending. If she touched them they would be like ashes in her hands. The vessel must be strong. If the vessel is not strong, it will break. Instead of peace, there will be only madness.

Pearl had had a baby. She had named the baby Sam.

She had no baby. She had lost the child because she didn't believe in it. Now there was only this other Sam ... this intimation ... a product of her understanding.

She had no one but herself. The gone child in herself.

Herself. A little child asking, insistent, of such an insistent child. *Would you love me if I was someone else? Would you ...* She had been a child. She had buckle shoes and a rabbit called Witch Hazel. The rabbit died. A violent death, as they say. The way all rabbits die.

Would you love me if I was ... Hush, Pearl. What a silly question. If you were another, you wouldn't be our Pearl. Now isn't that so? Hush ...

As a child she had believed in phantoms in the fire. She found that she could dismiss and summon them. She could tell them to go and they would go. But then when she grew older, she stopped believing in them and they would not go when she told them to go, and sometimes they would come when she didn't tell them to come.

Poor Pearl. Pearl ...

It is all one long day, a summer day, a day of thirst with the glass emptying, the children playing, then gone . . .

She had had a baby but the baby had died. It had fallen like a star from the sky. And then there was Sam, who had never been a baby, but something she had witnessed, and was now not even a child, but something charged to continue God.

Pearl wondered if they had been frightened, not in seeing Sam, who they knew, but in realizing the old woman, whom they had never seen. The hunter, the fisher of men.

She saw a terrible figure threading a hook through the body of a child, beginning at the groin and ending at a point near the eye. The child thrashed and struggled. The child was Jesse turning into a fish that couldn't swim away.

Pearl raised her fingers to her face. Luminous beetles crawled across the greenhouse glass. The interiors of their bodies were incandescent. They crossed and recrossed in every direction, appeared and vanished, were brought into creation and just as quickly annihilated. Pearl put her fingers closer to her face and saw her hands floating, illuminated in ashen light.

She saw the hunter setting the snares, the child running toward them, avoiding the first, clearing the second but then falling, something snapping in the child's soul. The child was Trip looking up with eyes like fat green flies.

Terrible, terrible. Pearl couldn't catch her breath.

"Pearl?" The door had opened. Thomas was standing there. "Pearl," he said. "What are you doing? Where are the children?"

Pearl's teeth chattered. Her body felt plunged in ice. Her body felt bruised and still and heavy suddenly with cold. The air she gasped for was like soup poured boiling down her throat. Thomas came toward her. He seemed illuminated by insects. The dead vines on the floor crackled beneath his feet. He helped her up and pushed the hair back from her face. Her face was smudged and wet. She'd been crying. He kissed her.

She did not move back. His tongue felt strange and hard. He pressed her body closer. What was it like for him? she thought. Breasts pressing against his chest. Spilling against his chest like guts falling from an animal, nipples nudging with their blind eyes . . . So much the difference between men and women. As between raw and cooked. As between wet and dry. And yet not enough.

Once when Peter and Trip were playing on the porch, she heard Trip say to her, "Uncle Thomas doesn't have a pecker, Pearl . . ." But it hadn't been pecker at all that he'd said of course, it had been checker. They had been playing checkers on the porch.

Her jaws ached with the kissing, but she didn't move, didn't resist. Why was he kissing her? She couldn't help him. Did he think she could help him? He ran his hand across her small breasts, across her boyish belly. She once believed that he was the one in charge, that he was in control, but he wasn't. No one was in control. Her own hands hung at her sides. His man's mouth was kissing her. Her own was filling with saliva. She wasn't doing it right. She felt excited and angry. She had forgotten how to do it. But one doesn't forget a thing like that. It's just that one doesn't want to anymore. She watched herself being kissed. She felt so far away, so many years away, watching this man and woman kiss, as though she had awakened to a previous dream.

He pushed his hand beneath her dress, his fingers now between the fold of panty and moist lip, rubbing into her. Her knees began to buckle but he caught her, bringing her softly down again to the floor. There was an occult smell, an earthy smell. Her body felt pleasure but her mind did not. Her mind was running off, shambling, horrified, a humpbacked child, running. She saw the little animals upon the table, in a circle, one. What outlaws they had been. Emma's children, what angels . . . making joy from their darkness, their eyes, the eyes of animals, every one, the smiles upon their lips, the smiles that changelings smile.

She was on her back. He dropped his face from hers and buried it between her legs. He pushed her back and up, heaved her legs around his neck, stroked her with his tongue from the crown of cunt to cleft of buttock. She cringed beneath him like a cone of paper in flame, and like a paper, too, fanned out, grew delicate and rose, all one with its disintegration.

She fluttered there, trembling with the softly ragged strokes of his tongue. Then he pulled away and pressed his mouth again on hers, pressing upon her lips the smell of herself, swamp smell, moon smell. She shuddered, her mouth filled with his milking of her, breathed in his breath and felt herself stiffening, coming. But then, abruptly, just before ending it stopped, the coiling rising. She moaned, repelled by it all. She had tried so earnestly once to be sane. But sanity, it was like holding onto a balloon, a balloon of the world, fragile and full of petty secrets and desires. She would let it go. It was easy to let it go.

His hands were by her head now, holding back her hair, trying to calm her, saying words to her. His bare, muscular arms held her, but all she could think of were the bones in the arms. She struggled. The thin table shuddered but stood, the little animals shuddered and flew off with no sound at all. She wrenched sideways, her lips finding the hand that lightly held her neck, catching the hand in her mouth and biting down with all her might, into the hand's heavy flesh, touching bone. He rolled from her with a cry and she scrambled to her feet and ran.

Outside, the trees made a sound like water falling. The lightning high above her made the sky look like the inside of a cave.

CHAPTER SIXTEEN

Pearl tried to shut out everything except the meadow through which she was running. The meadow ran to the unrisen stars. The wind had the time that was left in it and pushed against her face. The wind pushed the remembered children's remembered voices up from the bottom of her heart.

Look at me, Pearl! I can touch the bottom. I can touch the bottom of the pool!

Doesn't the sky look like a cave sometimes, Pearl? I'd hate to fall down through it. In England once a man was lowered down a place, the Eldon Hole they called it, seven hundred and seventy feet down he went and when they drew him up he was a raving maniac and died in seven days.

Don't go Pearl you're always trying to go listen the earth is like us you can hear it breathing listen he drank up all the water he ate up all the soap and he died last night with a bubble in his throat you will live but I will die if I can I will come back to you to you to you love you Pearl swing me over the rocks and I'll fly I won't cry who's the lady with the alligator purse is she bad is she good is she you Pearl they used to bury the dead in trees but the animals would come down from the bottom and go up from the top Peace in Rest they don't really go away when you do it backward like that you know those brandies where they have the fruit inside hanging there it's awful the peaches the pears the lunar hare Timmy loves honey the bees sting him and sting him but he doesn't care and

look at Peter he had a dream that a tree made feathers instead of
leaves in the springtime he used to say blatet for blanket can you
remember and he used to say yap for lap he never did his every
hour invented his face white as the pool smoking in the morning
do you know the Devil has six eyes to weep from here's a pretty
label it's got the Queen of England on it Pearl you be our Queen
and we will be your subjects we will stay here forever once I wet
my bed dreaming I was a wolf I saw the meadow the way a wolf
would see it it was nice I didn't know anything about me they say
that if a wolf pisses on you you have to follow him wherever he
goes tell us a story tell us about Sam look at that pompous sunset
isn't it pompous once I saw a sea horse a boy had it in a bucket
once I saw Miriam go into the house that has the sign of the lob-
ster upon it yes she goes to a medium in town it's a green house
the color of tamale Miriam talks to her she's going to let Miriam
talk to Johnny I feel funny Pearl look at my tooth isn't it a funny
tooth look at that clock it's trying to tell time Uncle Thomas says
that Time is the Tiger that eats us but that we are the Tiger too
I'm growing like the light grows see your heart's as big as the fist
you can make he used to say piddow he never did he never spoke
there weren't the words he knows from where we came and where
we are going and how we will return by another path after many
days we'll take care of you Pearl we love you drink this wine is a
wonderful thing wine a wonderful moment when water looked
upon its Maker and blushed as Milton said if Tracker killed his
daddy would God call him back would he have to go to school
Pearl your eyes have skinny cracks in them Emma's eyes were
like that skinny cracks through which the sunlight fell burning
falling was it true that that horizon spoke to you Emma was nice
she loved them too she could be pretty she could be whatever she
thought who twinkle twinkle little star what you say is what you
are Shelly says she's going to call the new baby Twinkle no mat-
ter what it is she's getting too old for that sort of thing grownups

aging get sort of soft and rotten don't you think they get mean hit him with a stone Timmy a thinking stone make a noodle of him stones have thoughts too though crabby ones everything has thoughts leaves discourse upon disintegration and water reflects upon the crudities of fish it's true but grownups are mean they eat meat they hit you in their sleep they tell you things they don't believe Uncle Thomas took Johnny out in the woods to punish him that's a pretty one Pearl but not this no don't buy that see the bird in the corner by the importer's address the bird with sorrow in its beak don't let's bring that one home with us Pearl stay with us there'll just be you and us

Pearl was staring into the pool at the body floating there. It was Shelly, her long hair loose and streaming. The water stirred and rocked gently against her legs canting down. Her head bumped against the grid beneath the diving board.

They're dying, Pearl thought. They're dying and there's nothing I can do. Pearl touched the canvas of the diving board and then in a queer spasmodic movement began touching her own lips and teeth and eyes. The water was a dark shade, impermanent but devastating and the other woman's body rocked lightly upon it.

I will tell Lincoln, Pearl thought. Lincoln will do something. He will breathe into her mouth. She will swim away laughing. The child will be born, the spitting image of its father.

Pearl ran across the grass toward the sauna. The door was open. Vapor poured into the air. She saw Lincoln on the floor slippery with wetness and hair. One eye pressed downward. The other rattled like paper. It shook in his head. The eye in darkness, already excluded from the world. She saw him dead, the blood upon his mouth like a wide purple flower. Everything was vivid in the heat. The color of the towel the corpse had rolled its haunches from. The smell of the cedar wood, the color of the ferns that grew from the cracks in the shower stall. A mottled lizard on a black stone held the remnants of another lizard in its mouth.

Pearl saw Lincoln's body's leg flung out, the muddy tracks across the shoulders, the sarcastic tongue stilled and thrust between the rigid lips, the tongue, that red and pointed organ more dangerous than the prick, protruding unwittily toward the corroded stall. She looked into the jelly of the dead man's eye. It had made its arrangement. Death is an arrangement like any other that one makes with the likes of oneself. He seemed unimaginatively wrought, dry, red, a pimple plump upon his buttock. Pearl sweated. It was terrible. But there were things more terrible than this. Pearl knew them.

Pearl saw prints in the long wet grass leading from the door into the trees. She could hear the moaning there of the children, the scolding murmurous cries, and she could see the darkness of the tree line shift forward with their passage through it.

The woods were like dark lace.

She could see the children threading through the woods.

She saw them, the patterns of their coats, the symmetry of their design. She saw their sparkling points of incorruptibility like the shapes of the stars just now blossoming in the heavens.

She saw herself running parallel with the children toward the house. Her tired legs pumped across the ground through the new night still faithful to the secret that it held. A star fell leaving a hole behind it. Lights spilled from the house. It smelled of mice and spilled liquor. Had she never noticed that before? And unseen timbers that never dried. She could hear the children panting, in a stream beside her. The house had all its endless rooms lit, the rooms that Aaron had made to keep the darkness out. One might as well live within it. He had built the rooms with his own hand, a frightened carpenter, one door constantly repeated, leading or locked to another, in the past, one hundred years ago, performing those irrevocable acts of the past, the memory of which time is made.

The sky splintered soundlessly open, breaking like the shell of an egg. For an instant she thought she might be able to see right into it. She came so close ... but she did not want to make anything up. She would not cheat. It was too late to cheat and she had come too far.

She reached the porch. Leaves lay upon the raw boards. A child's sweater slumped upon a wicker rocker. In the house, flowers rattled in a vase as the wind came in after her. She saw Miriam. At first Pearl was relieved. I'll have to tell her, she thought, and what she'd seen shaped spherical in the air between them.

I'll tell her, she thought.

She was relieved to see her there, to recognize the warm brown eyes, the face that grieved, the hands that nourished, the familiar skirt with its mooncalf language.

There was a radio playing. It pushed in on Pearl's thoughts. There was a broadcaster on it with a whining conspiratorial voice. It was close to her, just inside the kitchen. She turned it off. It made a click.

It was a sound like the old woman's looking at her. Pearl had heard it. In the head, a membrane floated across the eyes and then rose again with a click. Like the sound of a door being opened.

She heard a baby crying.

"It's Angie," Miriam said. She was fumbling with the stove. The stove didn't seem to be working. "You'd better go look at her."

I should tell her, Pearl thought. I will tell her the truth of this house. This house is in our minds. Truth is separated from Life very cunningly.

She passed through the kitchen toward the sound of the baby's cry and found Angie in the library wedged beneath the pillows of the sofa. Angie wept as though something was tearing her up inside. She held her arms out to Pearl.

Her legs are hurting her, Pearl thought. She picked her up and felt the child's damp, heavy bottom through her dress. It was a long party dress, red and white check, with a large gay bow in front.

Pearl kissed the child's hair, which smelled rank, and rocked her in her arms for a moment.

Angie stopped screaming and was now looking calmly up into Pearl's face.

They've left us behind haven't they? Pearl thought. The two of us. She looked into the child's innocent and inaccusable face.

The child was quiet but panting slightly. The room was quiet. Pearl's mind was calm. They'll blame me, she thought. But it doesn't matter. What does it matter?

"Look," Miriam was saying, "I want you to look."

For the children, she was saying. They can't be found.

Put that down, she was saying.

Angie's hair was wet as rags from crying. Pearl mopped at it with her hands. She started crying again. Pearl couldn't hush her.

"They are hiding," Miriam was saying. "They are playing a joke on us."

The food is cold. It's dark. It's beginning to rain.

"She must be sick, crying like that. I'll heat her some milk," Miriam was saying. "They've frightened her. I don't know what's gotten into them, playing such games."

I've had my own reversals today, Miriam was saying. That woman is a fraud. She asked for more money. I've given her so much. It's impossible for me to give her any more money. She said she saw my Johnny crying and running away from us because I had lied about something as petty as money. She said I had done the worst thing on this earth. I had betrayed a child's faith. She ordered me to leave. She had me so upset. I thought she might have me arrested.

Miriam was pale. A brown vein throbbed near her eye. She raised her hand to still it. Her arm was very white, too white, like the neck of a swan.

"Sometimes I thought I felt his eyes," Miriam was saying. "They were bright loops tightening around my heart. But she says now he won't look upon me anymore. He's turned his eyes away."

Pearl could hear the rain begin. She heard the green leaves lying on the ground one upon the other and the rain falling upon the rain. She could hear the rain falling on the faces of the children, upon their shells, taking them back, chrysalis-like, transferred.

I'm going to make another cup of tea, Miriam was saying. I can't seem to calm myself.

She went away. Angie pulled on Pearl's face.

"Here, here," Pearl said aimlessly. The child's eyes flickered. She wrinkled up her lips in a laugh.

The room smelled of perfume and cooking and the rain. And there was the overwhelming smell of liquor. Pearl left Angie on the couch and went to the bar where she poured herself a glass of gin.

She bent over Angie once more. A sourness rose in the back of her throat. The dress fell over the baby's feet. Pearl pushed it up. Angie's legs were withered and hairy, ending in sharp little claws. A thick, sorrel-colored tail flecked with gold fell down between the legs. The stomach was speckled and flat.

Pearl held Angie and went upstairs to her room. All the lights were on. Nothing had been disturbed. She made a little bed for Angie by putting two chairs together, then she slowly undressed herself and put on a nightgown. The gown had been hanging in the back of the closet for years. She seldom wore it. It was white with a hem of salmon-colored lace. She locked the door and slowly drank her gin.

It wasn't long before she heard the children softly scratching on the door.

"Pearl," they said, "where is everybody? Are they hiding? Where are you?"

I'm here, she said.

Once she had thought that she was crazy and that she might get well. She thought that she had to be herself. But there was no self. There were just the dreams she dreamed, the dreams that prepared her for her waking life.

"Come out, Pearl!"

Not yet, she said.

The children had their lives too, new forms by which the future would be accomplished.

She drank the gin. She was the drunkest person in the world. Inside she was bathed in crystal light. She turned off the lamps. She lit two candles, the second from the burning wick of the first. She watched her own simple gesture entranced. Then she blew the candles out.

Outside her now was a profound darkness that reminded her of the crystal light inside. She closed her eyes. The children went away. She was on a lost and drunken ark. There was no oar, no sail, no rudder . . .

Then they were back, whispering.

"Pearl, Miriam's in the kitchen. She's lying on the floor. She won't move. Her face is funny. It looks all collapsed."

They nudged at the door. The knob rattled.

The glass was almost empty. She could not bear to finish the last of it, to truly empty the glass. She held it with both hands. It is the guilt alone that matters, she thought.

Not yet, she said, I can't come yet.

"What shall we do about Miriam? She doesn't know what to tell us to do. Ashbel's scared. Franny's scared." Their voices were heavy and blurred.

In death we are not human and there is no need to know, Pearl thought.

She was on a lost and drunken ark. Her mind shuttled to and fro, dipped and rose, like water, sickeningly.

It will be all right, she said.

The wind sucked at the windows.

"Pearl!"

I'll be there, she said.

They were quiet. They went away. Pearl sat in the dark, but with the glass in her hands she held the last of the light and in herself she felt the inner morning.

Angie snuffled and stirred in her sleep.

Once they had been children, tamed by the years and her confusions. But now they were free and in that freedom was change and endless rebirth. She had brought about that freedom. Seven years ago she had brought here the instrument of change.

To take the leap! To fall. The fool. The dog.

Her mind shied, lingered.

The spirit is animal, she thought. It is the spirit which knows God. It is His favorite, His dream, freed from His imagination. The shadow of Jesus, the shadow of the Devil were so long ago laid to rest, side by side, in one common death, but the spirit is changeling. And is forever being fashioned into endless and impending transformations.

She raised the glass and drank, and felt herself being taken up by, being part of, an enormous wave just about to fold, just about to begin its long, triumphant fall . . .

The world seemed red. In the wave was the sky and she saw a great wine-colored falcon wheeling out of that sky, holding a rabbit in its pitying, merciless claws.

And then black, the wave, dissolving the black room. The peg-joined floor boards black, the single fly drowned in the dark glass, the curtains black against the night like loathsome angels, the black small shape on the chair.

Then white. Lovely it seemed. She lay quietly, looking. Galaxies of energy emptying light. But then a howling came out of it. The force of the vital shapeless wave drew back and up into its frightful cry.

"Bitch!" Thomas' word was. Bitch bitch bitch.

Out of the wave, his shadow with its man's mouth opening

at her, cursing, grabbing her hair with its one hand, wrapping it around its fist, while the other hand struck her face, peeled it back, and she could feel small bones fracturing softly in that face, of that woman so long ago.

There was a crash. Glass fell like stars. The wind beat against her ears like wings, great starved wings. Pearl screamed. "Bitch!" the word was. "Lunatic!"

She screamed because the person she was had to. The person she was no longer would not scream. That person was going to die and what could be done about that? Nothing could be done about that. The man who was trying to beat her half to death before she died punched her and she felt everything go flat. He was talking to her. He wanted her to know why she was being punished. He would hold her by the hair and give her an openhanded slap and then he would wait for a while as though he wanted her to understand it and then he would slap her again. It was painful. She screamed. She had just had a baby, only a few days before, and she still hurt from it. She had had many babies and they were all difficult births, but she loved them all. It was terrible that this man would be hitting her right after she had her baby with the baby right here with her, probably terrified, probably sobbing, although she couldn't hear it in the din.

The man shoved her down and she tried to wrench herself away from the baby but the baby was not there. She was falling but perhaps the baby had fallen farther. She screamed.

She saw the children massed in the doorway.

She saw them just an instant before they leapt into the room and dragged the man down. The little one with the round dark head was first. He fastened himself upon the man's neck. The flesh bunched out between the teeth.

Another had his long thin face deep into the man's side. Another chattered and dug at his eyes.

A mist of blood blew upon Pearl's face. They were tearing

him apart. They bit in. They held. The larger ones were on his chest, striking his chest with their jaws with a flat sound. She saw a sliver of yellow bone, a hand severed. With his last strength, the man pushed himself off the floor a few feet. His face turned. Pearl saw it. Blood streamed down it. The eyes were shut, the lips displaced in ribbons. And then the face vanished. It sank beneath the foaming heads.

Pearl saw it being finished. She watched the haggard, snarling impossible scene and accepted it. She saw the animals, their mouths full of meat, the eternal consuming the corruptible. She heard the silence around them all, the silence of the storm stilled. The silence of no screaming or snarling or cry. Just the dip, pull and flick of those mixed monsters of God's abyss.

Pearl rose painfully to her feet. Her nightdress was torn. She touched her swollen face. On the threshold of the room she saw the old woman, the skinny old woman holding Sam in her arms. She was stronger, stronger than one could possibly imagine. Once upon a time there was a child who wanted to run away. Once upon a time there was a child that wanted to be a real child. Once upon a time she had had a child that hadn't been hers. He had never been hers, he had never wanted to be a human child, she had, a very long time ago, made it up.

But there they were.

She remembered the night with everyone dead and the dogs running around her. But of course not everyone was dead. You could not live in a world where everyone was dead.

She remembered the night when she fell. It was warm like this night and something terrible had happened like this night. There was a child who was never found.

The old woman looked at Pearl from far away. Her face had never been complete but there had always been a look of anger upon it. But that was not so now. The old woman was not angry at Pearl anymore. Pearl had been forgiven. The old woman was not flying around in Pearl's mind anymore, angry with her about the child, flying around in Pearl's mind with awful wings. The old woman had what Pearl had called Sam and would leave now. She had left Pearl the others. She had not left Pearl alone. Pearl was forgiven. Pearl was gone.

Outside, away from the carcass within. The others followed her. She crouched on the wet ground in the view that Pearl had so often witnessed from her room, from the flowered chaise behind the windows as she lay drinking. She was the view now, she was the drunken vision scarcely outlined in the darkness, the inchoate body of the dream, at last perfectly recalled.

She crouched there and they pressed against her, the warmth of night in their coats. She traced the deep horn of fur above their eyes, the hard caskets of their skulls. She smelled the different odors of their skin, felt their black scalloped jaws. They scrubbed the sour folds of their skin with their rough tongues. They unraveled her tangled hair softly with their nails. The air was still and fresh. The only sound was of the animals breathing in the summer night. The animals who were children.

Animals like little flowers with only the smallest threads as their roots.

Animals like little stars with their past lives flickering.

Animals part of one large animal of God, the heart pounding and never breaking.

It was a summer night. Always it was summer in the womanish, childish, animal houseshape of God.

CHAPTER SEVENTEEN

Puuuuurl Puuuuurl it's my turn let me let me! he's like a cyborg maybe don't cry Trip read about them a long time ago he says they'll use a brain to fly the brain of an unborn child is the perfect thing to use on an otherwise unmanned flying ship it can go everywhere it can know everything when he smiles it stops raining all over the world it's just a mirror there all greasy so greasy you could write on it the world is happening everywhere at once isn't it nice not there here it's gloomy there Pearl it's empty too the harm's been done they're not here no truly you're the only person here and you're with us the others live in a mad world in the midst of strangers you remember that the struggle to love to eat to beware truly don't be anxious we would never betray you there was some sort of explosion Tracker grabbed the first thing he could it was a book about metoposcopy imagine it had a picture in it of a naked woman all covered with moles let me it's my turn to feed Pearl today at night his initial is among the stars Jane's got worms she eats too many flowers listen to that noise now that is an old noise the lost without the underground river the lost without has been found within happy? wring out a rag and put it around her wrists she likes that to dream of grapes means children put that blouse on her if she's cold no the other one's gone Pearl it fell apart Miriam was going to put a part of it in one of her skirts but she couldn't there wasn't anything for the thread to go through to dream of falling means children at night we crawl into a head it's

not a bad idea it's cozy and dark it sleeps Franny's got the dainti-
est hands of any creature around she can open anything the face
our hands feel is our face no more and yet the sensation is the same
see? sing her the song she likes you know i couldn't sing a note
until the hawk flew out my throat the hymn ohhhhhhh he walks
with me and no she doesn't want it he wasn't very big but some-
times he seemed big ohhhhhh Tracker stop it you are so mean yes
Pearl you know us better than anybody you see us as we are and
we see you no it's not raining do you feel wet now once it rained
for so many days that the flowers began growing out of the ma-
chines i will tell your fortune animals are by their very nature
prophetical as you know yes you will live forever here with us
dolphins foretell hurricanes for example birds flying on your right
bring luck and manatees think they're mermaids they really do
Genesis Exodus Leviticus Numbers we are now up to Corinthians
I for the fourth time you'd think she'd get tired of it but she never
does do you Pearl she loves that book and the other one that
manual that came with the stove you'd think there might be some
aesthetic tension there no no it's all right here 15 behold I tell you
a mystery we shall not all sleep but we shall all be changed ohh
yes she likes that look at that smile where is the biggest bar in the
world do you think i bet it's in Atlantic City Death's a wagon rat-
tling down the boardwalk Pearl's not going to get on that old
wagon are you Pearl no there's no need we'll plant potatoes in the
spring Peter can make vodka it's easier on the stomach ohh she
thinks that's funny isn't that funny Pearl yes it's true manatees
think they're mermaids because the sailors told them so no it's
not spring yet are you cold then we can't get any closer Pearl we're
as close as we can get what do you say to a pickle that's one year
old no Pearl your heart can't be cold that's just poetry why does
the weigher of the hearts of the dead have the head of a jackal
happy birthday is what you say that's Timmy's joke she wants you
to make a face ohh that's fierce the face your hands feel is imagine

that poacher shooting at Timmy out of that helicopter poor little
Timmy he was scared half to death it was a terrible sound and that
other man that man that came by boat with a bow and arrow and
shot at Tracker that man had a face like an asshole there was re-
ally something wrong with it faces when they're your own are
complex matters Trip's for example that spot where the hair doesn't
grow the spot that's in the shape of a boy's face all its own do you
think it has its own dreams that boy's face? in sleep you know the
treasure is buried in the darkness to which all creature's go we're
safe here Pearl and we're safe there too that's the part that's special
it's my turn to brush Pearl's hair how long it's gotten how pretty
yes pretty eggzactly it's not just brown it's impossible to define its
color really so many colors in such bewilderment that it seems to
be none at all when Ashbel was little and he'd find a pretty place
you know the oak you could stand up in or the little broken bridge
over the marsh he'd always have to pee that was when he was a
child seeing the water i wish that when we saw something we could
taste and feel and smell it too that it was all one thing wouldn't
that save a lot of time i suppose that happens on the astral level
no of course we have all the time in the world and even if we didn't
we would still be like this all of us here with you happy birthday
happy as for there Peter saw it yesterday he poked about it's a mess
the books have mushrooms in them poisonous and spiders every-
where the doors won't shut they're swollen open and there are
puddles and moths the color of whatever they rest upon every-
thing's broken not a thing works the paintings are as fuzzy as
Angie's hair we'll go there in the winter maybe when everything
is icy and rackety but the sun is nice today feel the sun the words
they used to say are gone now on the side of the speakable are
human beings but beyond the speakable is the beginning of the
world Pearl Pearl? she knows that why that's just something you
know isn't it of course the house is just mud and bones Peter said
it's dead well it had its day Pearl's got the slowest smile don't you

love the way it spreads Peter walked around the roof all the air's been let out of it was the way it seemed the children gone don't cry you've made her cry again don't cry feel the sun it's summer you used to say drinking made you feel it was summer all year long no well something similar night and the water seem the same that's why Jesse's never minded the dark if you hug him you'll drown it's always been difficult to show him affection but in his dreams he's loved in his dreams he's a child being rocked being rocked but we're in the day now the sky's as white as bread all that is learned is remembered little by little the face of a stranger peers out of the faces of us all it happens all the time she wants more about the house all right the house well you can imagine what remains the porch remains and the chimney and the staircase rising there's a smell of gas which is not unpleasant look at that boat with the bluish-gray sail we had a boat like that once with a sail faded just so just the color of your eyes Pearl a pearly colored sail a beautiful still day isn't it the boat's not moving at all the sky is white the sea's like silk it's summer well you could look through the windows like the weeds do they flourish around emptiness you could see what the weeds see like looking through a veil almost the same grown people go away they're contrived they can't be counted upon they go away the devices of their bones accomplished curl up on her she wants that yes we're here Pearl with you night and day month and year run together and are at rest here in us in these shapes we've been given we're happy in them you're scratching her get down and sponge her off a little she's hot the fishline stretches from the great above to the great below Jesse knows we all know the fire's in the wood as they say the whole's unlike the parts that make it life's not it's little moments after all and Aaron was no one's father as you've said and yet without his presence those lives could not have entered us yes he suffered the fate of death for us that was how it happened she wants to know she never tires of it well it happened gradual well *you* saw we never saw *her* but we knew better for it she was complete for us him we played with it was easy enough you showed us how to begin once there was a child yes lap that spot there where she's hurt herself she chews on herself sometimes i think once there was a child who traveled with his grandmother who would not let him go sometimes the two traveled as a bird in the sky and sometimes they went on land as wild things and sometimes they traveled as human beings but within each was the other within the woman was the child which she would not let go and within the child was the animal the changeling who was eternal when they seemed the most human as a child as an old woman they were these other things apart flying on wings as a bird flies in the channels that bank and drift between life and death or walking as an animal walks along the ridges and through the caves that link one sense of being with another they came here yes you brought them she's hearing hard you can tell cool that rag again how pretty her hands lie in her lap like empty gloves you went away but you came back and they came with you we played with him he was like us more and more he got to be like us you said and we like him yes we ate we slept we played carelessly we were on a journey you used to be afraid we knew that of the simple things the children their toys the clock the cars with their sealed eyes the water speak monotonously and calmly yes we're with you you know we love you speak calmly and rhythmically and softly the pump the screen the closed door the food on plates a ruin that house now a shell we don't live there anymore nature is generous and insensible the heart of heartlessness nothing endures or is completed everything is in constant change it happened gradual with the eyes first and then our bodies were no longer smooth and hairless down we went we fell to fours our heads were happy really we knew it could be done and it was done the way as you thought our enemies were defeated our head was like a house of keys tawny too crystal in a moment in a twinkling we were changed the children gone but us become in the instant of your cry don't spin it out too long she wants to curl up now help her grab our backs she's light as a feather look at the nice food Tracker found no not even a nibble? chew it up for her a little here you are then there that's better the lost without has been found we are your pets and protectors the circle is closed and we are with you there that's it quiet now there are no words for what you think Pearl there are no words for us words turn back Puuuuurl

Joy Williams has won the Rea Award for the Short Story, and the Harold and Mildred Strauss Living Award from the American Academy of Arts & Letters, among other prizes. Her first novel, *State of Grace,* was a National Book Award Finalist. Her most recent novel, *The Quick and the Dead,* was a finalist for the Pulitzer Prize.

OTHER PUBLICATIONS
BY FAIRY TALE REVIEW PRESS

Fairy Tale Review
The Blue Issue (2005)
The Green Issue (2006)
The Violet Issue (2007)
The White Issue (forthcoming, 2008)

PILOT ("Johann The Carousel Horse")
POETRY
By Johannes Goransson
ISBN 978-0-9799954-1-5

Changing: A Novella
FICTION
By Lily Hoang
ISBN 978-0-9799954-2-2